*Heartbeat for the World*

# HEARTBEAT
# FOR
# THE WORLD

### THE STORY OF
### GUSTAVE AND PAULINE WOERNER

*by Lorene Moothart*

**Christian Publications**

CAMP HILL, PENNSYLVANIA

Christian Publications, Inc.
3825 Hartzdale Drive, Camp Hill, PA 17011
www.cpi-horizon.com

*Faithful, biblical publishing since 1883*

ISBN: 0-87509-818-5

99 00 01 02 03    5 4 3 2 1

Cover portrait by Karl Foster
Photos supplied by Ruth Woerner Good

Unless otherwise indicated, Scripture taken
from the Holy Bible: King James Version.

# Dedication

To all students who sat under the teaching of Gustave and Pauline Woerner—in South China, Indonesia, Malaysia and Toccoa Falls College, including their three children: Robert, Ruth and Raymond, who in turn answered the call of God to go to the mission field.

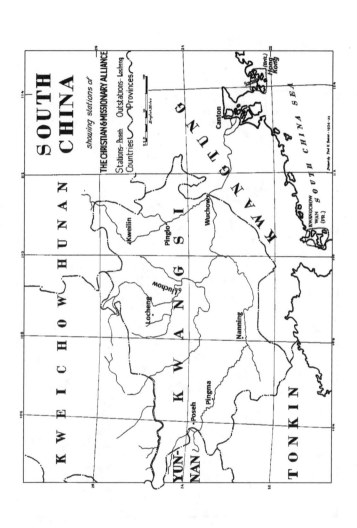

SOUTH CHINA

showing stations of

THE CHRISTIAN & MISSIONARY ALLIANCE

Stations-Poseh    Outstations-Locheng
Countries            Provinces

English Miles

Drawn by Ted K. Bawl 1934-'35

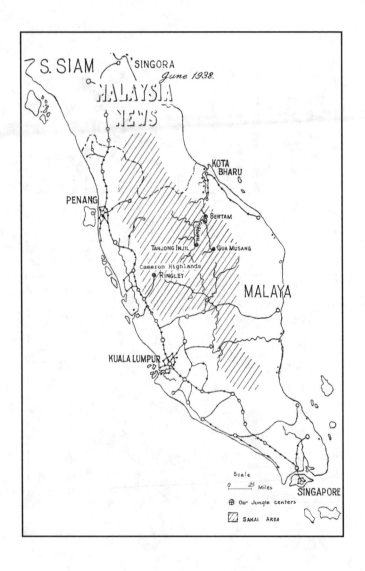

S. SIAM

SINGORA

*June 1938.*

MALAYSIA NEWS

KOTA BHARU

PENANG

Bertam

Plenong

Tanjong Injil

Gua Musang

Cameron Highlands

Ringlet

MALAYA

KUALA LUMPUR

Scale

0 ___ 25 Miles

SINGAPORE

⊕ Our Jungle centers

▨ Sakai Area

# Contents

# Foreword

Gustave Woerner was a missionary, a teacher, and, above all, a man of God. When I came to study missions at Toccoa Falls College, Uncle Gus was the missions professor. He was not a young man even then, but age never dimmed his zeal for reaching the world with the gospel of Jesus Christ. In his long missionary career he devoted a good part of his own life to reaching that world; then, through his students who became missionaries, his vision reached out to the ends of the earth.

I remember our classes singing "From Greenland's Icy Mountains" nearly every time he taught.

I remember him bouncing on his toes as he emphasized the needs of the people around the world yet unreached with the gospel.

I remember the Chinese characters he used to illustrate gospel truths.

Most of all, I remember the vision he imparted, not so much in the content of his classes, but in the burning desire of his heart to reach people for Christ.

When I came home from missionary service in the Middle East to teach missions at Toccoa

Falls College, my one prayer to God was framed in words similar to those of Elisha to his mentor, who was about to be taken to heaven: "Lord, give me a double portion of the spirit of Uncle Gus."

I trust God that Gus looks upon his spiritual legacy in the School of World Missions at Toccoa Falls College with a joyful heart.

Norman E. Allison, Ph.D.
Director, School of World Missions

# Preface

Seldom found in either secular or spiritual circles is a man as sold out for God as was Gustave (Uncle Gus) Woerner. Dedicated to God when very young by his mother, Gus' one purpose in life was to gather souls into God's kingdom. To read his life story is an inspiration indeed.

Even as a small child, and later as a youth, the word "missionary" moved Gus to pledge his life to win the lost, especially those who had never heard the words of eternal life.

"Not I, but Christ" (Galatians 2:20) became Gus' motto, along with the hymn "The Regions Beyond."

And go he did. Driven by his intense desire to reach those in South China, Indonesia and Malaysia, he pioneered in the far-flung outposts of those countries.

Gus has been labeled "a missionary for all seasons." When World War II forced him and his wife Pauline out of the Far East, he became a missionary at Toccoa Falls Institute (now Toccoa Falls College) as a faculty member. The Woerners preceded the author by one year.

For a time we lived in Gate Cottage; they had an apartment on the second floor; I, a room on the same floor. I also had the privilege of teaching their three children, both in high school and in college.

From the first meeting with Gustave Woerner, it was obvious that he put God first always. "Not I, but Christ" exemplified his walk with God, whether on the mission field or in the classroom. His prayers lifted those who heard up to the throne of God.

Pauline, his life's partner, should not be overlooked. She was at her husband's side on the mission field, nobly carrying a variety of responsibilities. In North America she engaged in missionary tours and participated in many aspects of campus life at Toccoa Falls. Her children "rise up and call her blessed."

Much of the material in this book has been taken from Gus' autobiography. Other sources include information provided by their daughter Ruth Woerner Good, and articles and letters written by the Woerners and published in *The Alliance Weekly, The Pioneer* (an Indonesian Mission publication) and *Malaysia News*.

May I express my special thanks to Suzanne Rich for her excellent suggestions and to Ruth Good for her help in making this book possible. Especially helpful has been the valuable editorial assistance of Angela Ramage and Marilynne Foster, the editor of the Jaffray Collection.

Thanks also goes to Gracie Cutts and to all who helped, encouraged and prayed for this book to become a reality.

Lorene Moothart
Toccoa, Georgia
October, 1997

# 1

# *If Not . . .*

Katherine stood motionless, the letter crushed in her hand—her hopes, her ambitions crushed too. Mechanically, she pushed the post office door closed and stumbled into the sunlight.

Gasping in the fresh air, she felt her legs give way as though they were rubber. She dropped heavily onto a bench nearby and sat there a long time, thinking, thinking, thinking. . . .

Katherine Kleiber had come from a little town in Germany called Adolsfurt, Württemberg, a village of about 300 inhabitants, too small even to have a post office. She remembered at times accompanying her sister's husband Karl Woerner to the town of Ohringen about four miles away. There, six days a week, he picked up the mail, put it into a padlocked box and walked back to Adolsfurt where he delivered it to the addressees in the evening. During the day, Karl would, with the help of the family, till about nine acres of land located in small, isolated patches surrounding the town.

For young Katherine, the excursions were a way to get out of the house and to delight in the scenery, particularly the small estate called Burghoff (literally "watchtower farm"). This estate, situated near the top of a gently sloping hill, commanded a magnificent view which centered on the city of Ohringen with its towering castle. The Woerner home nestled at the foot of Burghoff Hill.

But Katherine was unhappy here. Her older sister had married Karl Woerner, and other teenaged girls from the area were migrating to New York City. At eighteen years of age, it was time for her to leave home too. Strong-willed and adventurous person that she was, she decided to head for that famous American city.

In New York, she managed to obtain work at A.B. Simpson's orphanage. It was there that she and two of her coworkers found Jesus Christ as Savior. All three young women felt the Lord's call to the mission field and had only now earned enough money to enter Simpson's Missionary Training Institute in Nyack.

*God really does want me to be a missionary, doesn't He?* Katherine asked herself hesitantly as she fingered the crumpled letter now jammed into her pocket. It was both a statement and a question, the answer to which was clouded in doubt and conflicting emotions. The appeal from home was urgent: Her mother and older sister Johanna were very ill, and Johanna's children needed care.

A few years earlier Katherine would have ignored the appeal. "That's just too bad," she would have said, or at least thought while shrugging off the request. "Let them get along as best they can." But now she was a Christian. Her values had changed. She knew what she had to do. She, Katherine Kleiber, would put her own desires aside and answer the call.

Awkwardly, the slender blond girl pushed herself to her feet, squared her shoulders and went to her room to pack.

Naturally, Katherine was keenly disappointed that she was unable to go to Nyack with her friends (all later became missionaries to the Far East). But because she felt that returning to Germany was God's will—at least for now—she bowed to it with acceptance.

After three years, Johanna died of tuberculosis. But Katherine was not free. She was still needed as nurse to her ailing mother and as housekeeper and mother to Karl's children. For four more years her mother lingered as an invalid before God released her to rest in her heavenly home. Now, after seven long years, perhaps Katherine could fulfill her dream. Or could she? She knew that by now she was considered too old to be an overseas missionary. Besides,

Johanna's husband Karl had asked her to marry him. She accepted.

Karl and Katherine Woerner were members of the Lutheran Church. They were very religious. Karl, as husband and father, was, of course, the head of the house; but in a truer sense, Christ was the head of the house, and family worship was faithfully observed mornings and evenings. From the Bible the children learned their responsibilities to each other: to honor Father and Mother and practice brotherly love among their brothers and sisters.

It was January 19, 1896, a bitterly cold day in a poor peasant's home in Adolsfurt, Württemberg, Germany; but excitement was in the air. Karl Woerner's four children, now teenagers, were anticipating the birth of a new baby in the family. When "It's a boy" was announced, they all rejoiced, and Gustave Woerner (or Gus, as he became known) was welcomed into the family. Katherine particularly was happy. *Could it be that God is giving me this son to go to the mission field in my place?* she wondered hopefully.

But Gus was not a robust child and was often ill. When he was about a year old, he began to have convulsions. In the weeks that followed, they became increasingly more frequent and painful. Katherine's pleading with the Lord for healing for her son seemed in vain. His condition did not improve, but rather grew worse.

One day, in despair and fearing that Gus would not live much longer, Katherine carried him up the ladder into the attic and placed him on a blanket on the floor. Sobbing what she thought could be her last prayer for her little son, she cried, "Lord, I cannot bear to look on his suffering any longer. Do what You wish: take him home or, if not, make him a missionary."

Tenderly she placed the child in the hands of God and, resigned in her spirit, slowly crawled down the ladder to attend to her many duties. Concerned as to how God might be answering her prayer, after her tasks were finally completed, she climbed back up the ladder. Imagine her surprise and great joy when she found her son sitting up, smiling and playing with some little potatoes that were stored nearby.

"Praise God!" Katherine cried out loud. "It's divine healing!" She was convinced that God had spared Gus to be a missionary. However, Gus was not immediately healed. Though not so severe, convulsions (probably a form of epilepsy) lingered throughout his youth. The attacks diminished as he grew older and had finally disappeared by the time he was recruited into the army.

Little Gus was a rather lonely child. Being anemic, he was not allowed outside during the winter months. However, since barns often joined houses in this little German village, Gus would struggle into his heavy coat, put on his cap and mittens and wander down the covered

passageway to the barn where he petted the
family cows. They were not only valuable for
their milk, but were also needed to pull the
wagon and the plow. A milk goat provided the
necessary nourishment for Gus.

It came as a real financial blow to the family
when one of the cows broke her leg and had to
be sold to the butcher. It was almost a year before they could get enough money to replace
her. The new acquisition turned out to be quite
unruly and difficult to control.

One day, as Gus' brother Harry led the defi-
ant cow to the village watering trough, she broke
loose and began to run wildly around the village
square. Spying Gus playing nearby, she made a
mad dash toward him and scooped him up with
her horns, shaking him furiously and finally
flinging him onto a pile of crushed rock. Fortunately, Harry saw it all and rescued Gus from
the cow's attempt to gore him to death.

Mother Woerner never sent Gus and his younger siblings—Carl, Martha and Gertrude—to
bed; she took them there. And she taught them
the Scriptures. Two verses became especially
meaningful: "Create in me a clean heart, O God;
and renew a right spirit within me" (Psalm 51:10)
and First John 1:7: "But if we walk in the light, as
he is in the light, we have fellowship one with another, and the blood of Jesus Christ his Son
cleanseth us from all sin." The focus of those
verses would, in an unusual way, become the fo-

cus of at least one of her children—namely, her
son, Gustave.

As time marched on, the four oldest children
joined thousands of others who sailed to America,
the land of opportunity. Their goal was not to
amass money for themselves, but to send it back
to Germany in order to bring the rest of the family
to America and be united once more.

Finally, when there was enough to purchase the
tickets, the Woerner family, amidst a flood of
mixed emotions, said good-bye to their German
family and friends and sailed for America. Katherine had been looking forward to this day with
great joy and expectation. Having been in America before, she knew where they were going, the
opportunities that faced them. Her years at the
orphanage and at the Gospel Tabernacle were
filled with happy memories. It was there that she
had accepted the Lord as her Savior. She was
looking forward to renewed spiritual blessings and
fellowship with friends.

But for Gus' father, it was different. He had
never been more than fifty miles from home except when he served in the Franco-Prussian
War. America to him seemed like the end of the
earth. He was already fifty-six and could hardly
give up his few parcels of land even though everyone assured him there was nothing to fear in
the new country. As for the children, they were
anticipating the upcoming venture.

At first the voyage was exciting, but soon the novelty wore off. Gus, just seven years old, began to fear the ship would never arrive at the harbor. Finally, one day, the passengers were told that the journey would end that night. New York was just hours away.

After supper, Gus rushed to the foredeck, but no land was visible. However, as darkness fell and the minutes ticked by, the welcoming lights of New York City came into view, then blazed on all sides of them as the ship dropped anchor. Within moments, the family was surrounded with joyful greetings. Gus' siblings from Germany—Lilly, Anna, Harry and Fred—were there among others. *Could I ever be happier in heaven?* Gus wondered to himself. The weeping, laughing and joy were unspeakable!

Only nine days after embarking on the *SS Kromland*, the Woerners found themselves the occupants of a "flat" on the fourth floor of 319 W. 39th Street in New York City. The transition time was none too long. The realities of the life in the new world had to be faced sooner than expected.

One of the most pressing demands was to register Gus in public school. Since he had completed half of his first year in Germany, he was placed in grade 2A. Although Gus' teacher patiently helped him to learn English and understand the words he was trying to pronounce, his greatest encouragement came from his mother's prayers. Every morning before the children left for school,

Mother Woerner knelt with brothers Carl and Gus and prayed that the Lord would protect them and provide wisdom for their lives. The second year, Gus was promoted to the third grade and before the end of that year was at the head of his class.

Father Woerner also assisted in his younger children's education. Since he had difficulty getting employment because of his age and lack of fluency in English, he often took Gus, Martha and Carl to places like the Central Park Menagerie, the Bronx Park Zoo, The Museum of Natural History and many other attractions, all of which proved to be very exciting for the wide-eyed children.

But the most thrilling of all was the escalator at the Macy's department store. Imagine standing on a moving stairway! The most troublesome incident took place when Father Woerner's wallet was stolen and the family had to walk the fifty blocks home!

One of the greatest sources of hope and joy for the family came from their attendance at Dr. Simpson's Gospel Tabernacle in New York City. During a revival meeting, sister Anna took little Gus. It was there that he first saw people going forward to an altar.

"Why are they doing that?" Gus whispered in Anna's ear.

"They want to confess their sins and ask God to take them to heaven when they die," she explained simply.

Fear gripped Gus' soul. *Surely then*, he thought, *if I die tonight, I'll go to hell*. Anna explained that Jesus loves little children and that He died for their sins too. Then she asked, "Will you let Jesus come into your heart, Gus?"

"Yes," he responded, though he wasn't sure what that really meant.

Two years went by. Then Katherine, who had been unwell for some time, grew very ill. Intense prayer did not seem to help. Finally, a friend of the family, a Christian physician, fearing tuberculosis, suggested they move to southern Alabama. The climate would be good for her, and besides, land was cheap.

After waiting on God for His direction, the four older children decided a move was necessary for their mother's sake. Since they knew nothing about Elberta, Alabama, the planned destination, they sent Fred, the oldest son, to "spy out the land."

Elberta turned out to be a small crossroads town in the southernmost part of the state. There Fred got title to forty acres of land, hired a couple of so-called carpenters, walked back the six miles to the train station carrying two suitcases and headed for home.

The family packed up their belongings and boarded a ship sailing for Savannah, Georgia. There, while waiting for the vessel to discharge and take on passengers and cargo, Gus and Carl decided to play tag on the pier. Their game was brought to an abrupt halt when Gus accidentally slipped on a banana peel and slid into the bay between the ship and the wharf. Carl screamed for help while Gus, unable to swim, struggled desperately for something to grab onto. He opened his mouth to pray, only to have salt water rush in as he once again slid beneath the waves.

*God, help me not to die!* he thought. Almost at once, he felt a hand grasping his arm and another hand lifting him onto the pier. Gus looked into his rescuers' faces, and in that moment was born what would become a deep and enduring love for black people.

The remainder of the voyage to Mobile was uneventful. After a train ride to Summerdale, the family bought an uncovered farm wagon and two horses, piled their earthly belongings and themselves onto the wagon and plodded, through darkness and rain, the last nine miles to their new home.

Life in Alabama was different—and hard. Money was scarce. One day a near-tragedy brought the doctor to the Woerner home. Five-year-old Gertrude had been hit accidentally near her heart by bird shot. The doctor, after taking a brief look at the little girl, headed for the door, announcing as he went, "You owe me $45."

Forty-five dollars! That was a tremendous sum of money. Through her tears, Mother Woerner sobbed, "We don't have money now to pay you." Before she could explain that one way or another the bill would be paid, the doctor interrupted.

"You mean to say you have no money in the house at all?"

"We have only a $10 bill, but it is tithe money that belongs to the Lord."

"Well, give me the $10 and we will call the account closed."

"We'll pay you later," Mother Woerner promised, "but the $10 is the Lord's money and I can't give you that." The discussion continued. Finally the doctor prevailed and took the $10 bill.

"Remember, it is the Lord's money," Mrs. Woerner said as she reluctantly handed him the payment.

Within an hour the doctor was back.

"When I opened my billfold to get the money, it was not there," he said with a perplexed look on his face. "I don't know where it could be."

Gus and Carl walked down the road looking for the money, but it was never found.

# 2

# *A Bicycle for God*

It was 1911. Fourteen years had passed since Gus' mother had prayed for her son in the attic in Germany. God had not forgotten her missionary prayer. Once more, He nudged Gus toward that end.

This time God's call came in the form of a headache which Gus endured for several days. Saying nothing to his parents, he went out as usual to work in the peach orchard, hoeing around the trees where the cultivator could not reach. But by the middle of this particular morning the headache had gotten so severe that he had to go back to the house.

Katherine felt her son's brow. Sensing the need for dependence on the Lord for healing, she said, "Go upstairs and read the Bible." *If God is going to speak to my son*, she thought, *He will surely do it through His Word.* Gus obeyed.

As he picked up his Bible, it fell open at the book of Esther. He began to read. It was so interesting that Gus soon forgot his headache and read the entire book. After a nearly untouched lunch, he went back to work, but the headache persisted. That night, he ate no supper and went straight to bed.

As soon as her work was done, Mother Woerner joined Gus in his room in the attic and once more, according to custom, prayed for him. With his head throbbing, all Gus could hear was "missionary, missionary, missionary." Kissing her son good night, Katherine retreated from the room. Alone with his pain, a familiar feeling rose in Gus' heart—the thought that he might die.

"If You heal me," he finally told the Lord, "I'll be Your missionary."

Sleep came quickly, as did the healing power of God. In the morning the headache was gone.

The next day *The Alliance Weekly* arrived in the mail. The featured report told of the opening of French Indochina to missionary work and the urgent need for preaching the gospel to its 25 million lost souls. Gus was so gripped with a sense of urgency that in a childlike way he knelt and prayed, "God, do You want me to be a missionary to this field?"

This was Gus' moment, his first personal, conscious step in dedicating his life for missionary service. He never forgot that promise to the

Lord, though he sometimes wondered, with good reason, *How can I ever go?*

The family continued to be very poor. Father was disillusioned about the soil, so poor and sandy compared to the heavy, rich soil of his few acres in Adolsfurt. Lilly, Anna and Harry had sent enough money with which to purchase the essential implements for the farm, but now a better house needed to be built. Fred "hired out" to neighbors within walking distance (one to seven miles!), and Carl and Gus helped their father at home. When Gus finished the sixth grade, his father took him out of school and hired him out too. His meager earnings could be added to the family coffers.

*How can I ever get the training I need to be a missionary if I can't finish school?* Gus wondered as the days, weeks and months flashed by. *God, it's in Your hands*, he finally prayed.

Soon Carl joined Gus in working on the neighboring farms.

"I hate having to walk so far to work," Carl grumbled one day as they once again set out for the neighbor's place.

"Yeh, there ought to be some better way," Gus responded.

Carl, deep in thought, kicked the stones and stared down the long road that stretched out in front of them.

"A bicycle!" he shouted finally. "We could buy a bicycle and take turns riding."

Gus agreed.

From that moment, the boys could think of nothing else. When the Montgomery Ward catalog came out that fall, they often spent their evenings, after prayers, sprawled out on the floor with the catalog between them, carefully studying the bike pages and discussing the advantages and disadvantages of the various models.

"Oh, Mother," they pleaded, "could you spare a little money each week until we can save up enough money for a bike?"

"I'll try," she promised, "but it won't be more than a few cents at a time." The boys worked harder than ever and talked every day about what it would be like when they got their bike.

It was March of 1913. The day started much like any other, except that this was the day of the week when *The Alliance Weekly* usually arrived. Even though it was a half-mile walk to the rural mailbox, both Gus and Carl wanted to be the one to go down the path, get the mail and hurry back with the precious magazine their mother enjoyed so much.

"Just think, Mother," Carl boasted, "it won't be long until we get the paper to you quicker. We'll have our new bicycle soon."

"I get the first ride. I'm older," Gus countered, exerting his big-brother rights.

Mother Woerner gazed fondly at her sons. Fine boys, both of them. They had worked so hard, saving nickels and dimes, one at a time.

Now they had managed to save $18. Only $8 was lacking until they could send the order to Montgomery Ward. Of course, it would be some time yet—$8 was a lot of money.

In return for very long working days, Gus and Carl received fifty cents a day, of which they could keep only ten to twenty-five cents a week, depending on how much their mother could spare. Meanwhile, they often turned to the back of the Montgomery Ward catalog where the bicycle of their dreams, a "Ranger," was advertised for only $26! They would patiently wait. And work.

However, the news in the newly arrived *Alliance Weekly* was tragic. In northeast Georgia, the stately building housing the Toccoa Falls Bible Institute had burned to the ground. It had been purchased only two years earlier by Rev. R.A. Forrest to be used as a Bible school, "a tree of God's planting," he had called it. Now, believing that everything possible must be done to rebuild and carry on the fledgling work, Rev. Forrest was making an appeal for help.

That evening at family worship, Gus' mother wept and prayed earnestly for Rev. Forrest and "God's Bible School" as she called it. Before he went to bed that night, Gus, now seventeen, read the article for himself. He too was greatly moved by Rev. Forrest's plea. He could not get the school off his mind.

"I want to do something, Lord, but what?" he prayed. The night passed slowly as Gus lay awake, staring at the ceiling and wondering what he could do to help the people at Toccoa Falls.

At the table the next morning, Mother Woerner told the family, "I feel led of the Lord to take the tithe money we have—it's $12 right now—and send it to Rev. Forrest. But what is that toward such a staggering loss and enormous need?"

All day Gus kept thinking of the $9 which was his share of the bicycle money. Finally, he decided to add it to his mother's tithe and send it to Rev. Forrest.

Mother Woerner was delighted with the decision, but Carl was appalled, even angry. He stumbled out of his chair and shot out the door, letting it slam behind him. Gus followed him.

"Carl, I'm sorry. I don't blame you for feeling bad, but I had to give the Lord my share."

"Yeah, you're giving up your money," Carl stormed, "but that means I can't get the bike either. I could never save up enough alone." He kicked a clod viciously.

Gus fought to hold back his tears. He didn't want to hurt his brother, but neither could he ignore the tug at his heart. When Carl saw the tears, he also started to cry. Salty tears mingled as the brothers embraced.

"All right, Gus, let's go tell Mother. I'll give her my share too. That'll make $30. Won't she be happy!"

When Mother heard the news, all she could say was, "Praise the Lord." Neither Karl nor Katherine could write in English, so Gus wrote the letter to Rev. Forrest. Then he walked the two miles to the post office and purchased a money order for $30.

This incident seems to have been a turning point in Gus' life, where it all began—a lifetime of devotion to the Lord, of putting God first, of following the words in Galatians 2:20: "Not I, but Christ." Of course Gus could not know that eventually he would serve Him at the very school to which he had donated his bicycle money. He had cast his bread upon the waters. He would find it after many days.

The following summer, Gus worked for the neighbors, a family by the name of Heil. Mr. Heil's younger brother also worked alongside Gus.

One day, Mr. and Mrs. Heil went away for the day. Before they left, Mrs. Heil hung the bedding out on the line to air.

"If it rains," she told the boys, "you be sure to take in the bedding before it gets wet."

"Yes, ma'am," they assured her. "We will."

About 10 o'clock clouds began to form and shortly after that the rain came. Near the edge of the field where the boys were working stood a lone pine tree about sixty feet tall and two feet in diameter. They ran there for shelter. Just as they crawled under the shelter of the branches, Gus remembered the bedding.

"We have to get the bedding!" he screamed above the thunder.

Making a dash toward the house, the boys had distanced themselves less than a hundred feet from the tree when a lightning bolt struck it, slicing off a slab of wood and hurtling it in their direction.

"Wow! That was a close one. It looks like the devil is out to get us," Gus gasped as they reached the clothesline and pulled the bedding into their arms. It was not until they returned to work that they realized the size of the piece of wood that had landed just behind them. It was twenty feet long and ten inches wide!

*What if we hadn't remembered our promise to Mrs. Heil and had stayed under the tree just a few seconds longer?* Gus thought. *Surely God was with us.*

Little by little, step by step, God was dealing with Gus about becoming a missionary: the time he promised God that if He would heal him he would be a missionary; the experience of giving up his cherished dream of a bicycle; and the miracle of protection from the evil intentions of the storm.

Gus was also influenced by the example of the members of his family. His older brother Fred became a model for Gus to emulate. He started a Christian and Missionary Alliance church in Elberta, organizing Sunday school classes and teaching them. When he left, Fred said simply, "Gus, you teach my Sunday school class and carry on as best you can with the Lord's help."

Scared and overwhelmed, Gus finally agreed.

Then, of course, there was the godly mother who prayed daily for her son. Gus had watched her live a consecrated Christian life despite poverty and deprivation. She never complained, but exhibited instead a spirit of thanksgiving and prayer. Even the specter of tuberculosis that had threatened her in New York City had disappeared.

And, finally, Gus thanked the Lord for the father who worked so diligently to provide for his family and who blessed his son with his last breath. His father died December 5, 1913.

Although worried about the fact that it was impossible for the family to buy an expensive coffin for Father Woerner, Katherine was disturbed about something else: Her husband had two suits, a threadbare one and a new one purchased only two months previously. Nearby lived an elderly couple who were so poor that the husband could not afford a suit at all and had to come to services at the church in worn overalls.

Mother Woerner gathered the family together.

"Children," she asked, "what should I do—bury Father in the new suit or give it to our neighbor?" After some discussion about "what would the neighbors think" and "didn't Father deserve to be buried in his new suit," Mother Woerner decided that no matter what others might think, the new suit would be given to the neighbor. Katherine's act of love and sacrifice made a deep impression on her son.

God also knew that the time would come when Gus would need a passport to go as a missionary. Just two months before his death, Father Woerner received his "second papers" which made him a bona fide citizen of the United States. According to law, the names of his minor children were inscribed on the backside. This automatically made them U.S. citizens also.

Though this meant little to Gus at the time, ten years later when he completed his training and applied for a passport to go to China, all he had to do was to present his father's papers to prove he was an American citizen.

"God doeth great things past finding out; yea, wonders without number," Gus murmured gratefully.

# 3

# *No Questions Now*

*L*ord, *how can I know I am Your child?* The question continued to haunt Gus' heart and mind. *You know that when I was seven I prayed to receive You into my heart. You know I've taught Sunday school classes since I was fourteen, and even sacrificed my bicycle for God's work, and that I've always been glad I did. Still, I'm not sure that I am a Christian. Should I give up my class? How can I continue teaching?*

These disturbing thoughts continued to surface in Gus' mind. He wondered if he was really born-again in the true sense of the word. He longed for the spirit he could see in his mother and brother Fred, but he felt frustrated. His life was becoming a treadmill of hoping for and trying to do his best. But a kind and loving heavenly Father, seeing the desire of His hungry child, set about to fulfill his spiritual longings.

With a heart made tender by the loss of his father, Gus began to be burdened for the salvation of all his Sunday school pupils. On New Year's Eve, the last Sunday in 1913, after dismissing his class, he went to his room to pray.

"Lord, I want my pupils to know You and love You, but how can I point them to You when I'm not sure I know the way myself?"

On a table by his bed lay a little pile of Christian novels Gus had unpacked, all of them entitled *The First Soprano*. He had ordered one for himself and the rest were to be given as awards to the seven students who had the best attendance. After concluding his prayer, he picked up a copy of the book and began to leaf through it. As he read, deep desire, interest and expectancy were born in his heart. It seemed he could see himself within the pages. He found a profound spiritual longing welling up in his heart to learn more of God's personal love and faithful nature.

From the midnight noise outside his window, Gus knew that the new year of 1914 had begun, but he could not put the book aside. The Holy Spirit began to show him more clearly how Jesus had died and shed His precious blood for him—Gus. Christ had chosen to die for his sins—past, present and future. All were covered.

As light dawned on New Year's Day, divine light shone into Gus' soul, bringing a new sense of assurance and peace such as he had never felt before. The following Sunday was one of the happiest moments of his life. He presented the books to his pupils, told them how the Lord had blessed his own heart and encouraged them also to be sure they belonged to Christ.

After Father Woerner's death, Gus and his mother were the only ones at home to run the farm. It was a great responsibility for a teenager and a frail mother. But Gus had a seed catalog that advertised a new type of seed corn that would yield three to five large ears on a single stalk! He persuaded his mother to let him order the seed and plant five acres.

As the spring rains and the rays of the sun moistened and warmed the soil, sturdy young shoots began to appear. The experiment looked promising. However, within days, a flock of meadowlarks attacked the field, uprooting nearly half the plants and devouring the kernels. Gus felt sick. That night his mother prayed that God would do something about it. Imagine their joy the next morning to find the meadowlarks gone. They never returned—and the crop turned out to be an exceptional one.

Soon after, Fred and his wife came back to Elberta to free Gus to join a group of young men who, beginning in Oklahoma, followed the threshing crews west and north until the season closed in Wisconsin. The trip was not without its own brand of excitement.

One day, while working on a farm in Oklahoma, Gus noticed some odd-looking clouds. Not giving them a second thought, he went to bed, only to be awakened sometime later with a violent jolt. A tornado had bulldozed its way through the farmyard, leaving a path of destruction about 300 yards wide, dismantling the barn and carrying the cattle away. Had the tornado hit fifty feet to the left, the house, with Gus and the other occupants, would have been in its direct path. Again, God had protected His child.

At the end of the harvest season, Carl asked Gus to move to Wisconsin. Their sister Martha joined them too. There they were all baptized in the local Baptist church, becoming not only brothers and sister in the flesh but in the spirit also.

What course Gus' life might have taken had the United States not declared war on Germany in 1917 will never be known. However, since he was now twenty-one, he was drafted into the U.S. Army. With this unhappy turn of events, instead of enrolling in Dr. Simpson's Institute in Nyack, Gus found himself in boot camp. But a deep and frightening thought was swirling in his mind: He didn't want to be classified as a conscientious objector, but (and he shuddered at the thought) neither did he want to kill anyone, particularly a German who could be one of his very own cousins! In a most unusual way, God providentially spared him from that.

While Gus was still in training, his battery was assigned to break the horses for pulling the cannons and caissons. All went without incident until it was Gus' turn.

He was sitting on top of the corral fence, watching the proceedings, when he noticed that most of the soldiers breaking the horses were large and heavyset. Since he was only five feet six inches tall and very slender himself, he wondered if he could handle so large an animal. Well, he would try his best! When his name was called, he stepped forward.

As Gus mounted his horse, it broke away from the two soldiers leading it. Gus found himself riding without bridle or saddle. Free of restraints, his mount galloped wildly toward a high fence, with Gus hanging on to his mane for dear life. Suddenly, the horse stopped. Gus was propelled over the horse's head and landed on the frozen ground on the other side of the fence. Bruised, bleeding and suffering a broken leg, Gus was unable to go when his division was shipped overseas. Once again, God's purposes for Gus' life were evident, for before he was dismissed from the hospital, he learned that nearly the entire division had been lost in combat.

Gus was a good soldier and well-liked by the other men even though they nicknamed him "Gloomy." At first this bothered him until he learned the reason for the name: Because he did not smoke, drink, play cards, roll dice, use profanity or vulgarity, or tell or listen to smutty stories, the other men perceived him as being gloomy. However, when the chips were down,

Gus was the one they called on to pray. And God always honored his prayers.

After his leg healed, Gus was assigned to a much smaller division and was eventually shipped to Britain and on to France. However, several weeks later, on November 11, 1918, the war ended. Gus' prayers to be spared from killing anyone had been answered.

During his stretch in the army, Gus felt his missionary call crystallize. His dream to attend the Missionary Training Institute in Nyack, New York, was about to come true. As soon as possible he requested to be transferred to "Casuals" and was honorably discharged.

"Nyack, here I come!" he shouted as though walking on air. "French Indochina, I'm on my way!" But, once again, there was a problem—Gus was short of funds. Even after combining his pay from the army with the money he received from cashing his Liberty Bonds, he still did not have the amount needed to register at Nyack.

With his brothers and sisters taking on the care of their mother, Gus took a job at the National Cloak and Suit Company, working as a stock clerk. True to his conscientious and self-disciplined bent, Gus was soon promoted to a salesman's position. He did so well that he was able to purchase all the clothes he needed at greatly reduced rates. Months later, after three raises and now the proud owner of an entire wardrobe, Gus had the money he needed to attend Nyack.

"If you'll stay with us," his employers told him when he resigned, "we'll raise your salary from $24 to $60 a week."

"Thank you, that's a most attractive offer," Gus responded gratefully. "But I'll have to refuse." He already had a commitment to a higher authority that would take him thousands of miles from family and friends. Nothing had ever impacted or ever would impact his life like his decision to follow Christ.

"This is a training institute, with emphasis on 'training,' " the registrar said firmly when Gus enrolled. Gus got the point. He studied diligently to make up for his lack of formal education. It wasn't long until he qualified for the regular courses. Although he enjoyed his studies, the passion of Gus' heart was to get the gospel to people. So he organized street meetings, volunteered at the city rescue missions and the Sunday morning services for sailors, and visited the local hospitals telling people about God's plan of salvation.

At the Institute, the students organized what they called "Noon Prayers." Gus was chosen as their leader each of the three years he was there. He also was asked to assist in worship services at a small church in Glen Cove, Long Island. As God would have it, he became the pastor, a position he held throughout his time at Nyack.

With life so busy, Gus contemplated dropping some of his responsibilities. Not really wanting to do that, instead he decided he would skip his noon meals and use that time to read his Bible and pray. One day as he read the story of Jesus in the Garden of Gethsemane, he was struck by the words, "He went a little farther" (Matthew 26:39).

"That's it," Gus cried out loud. "I'll not drop anything, but I'll go a little farther, and God will give me strength to do it." That response of his heart is captured by the following thoughts he put on paper:

> Are you sorely pressed by trials?
> Do you say I can't endure?
> Just remember in the conflict,
> Only fire makes gold pure.
> Do not chide with God your Father,
> "Jesus went a little farther."

It seemed to Gus that the three years he spent at Nyack flew by more quickly than any other three years of his life. Toward the end of the third year, the senior class voted to adopt a class motto: "Not I, but Christ" (Galatians 2:20). In response to a public request, Gus, among others, submitted a poem and a song to go along with the theme. Both of his entries won first place. The chorus of his song, "Not I, but Christ," read:

Not I, but Christ; Not I, but Christ,
My constant prayer shall be.
Oh, crucify each vain desire,
And live Thy life in me.

The phrase became Gus' life theme.

Near the end of his senior year, when Gus applied to the Alliance Foreign Mission Board for missionary service, it just so happened that Dr. R.A. Jaffray, chairman of the Indochina field, was home on furlough and was interviewing applicants for that field. Since Gus had filed his request for French Indochina, Jaffray agreed to meet with him.

It didn't take long for Jaffray to note Gus' name.

"German?" he asked, shaking his head.

"I'm an American citizen, but I was born in Germany," Gus responded.

"Then I'm afraid that disqualifies you. It's too soon after the war. French Indochina would never accept a German."

The news hit hard. Tears brimmed unbidden in Gus' eyes.

"Oh, don't give up," Jaffray responded kindly. "You can still go to the Far East as a missionary. Remember, God didn't send Adoniram Judson to his choice, India, but to Burma. Robert Morrison wanted to go to Africa, but he was sent to China. And David Livingstone chose China, but God sent him to Africa. Leave the decision as to where you will go in the hands of God and the Mission Board."

Gus agreed. He was eventually appointed to South China, the field headed by Dr. Jaffray. Gus couldn't have been happier. But there was one problem. The convulsions he suffered as a child had returned. Questions flooded his mind and brought deep darkness to his soul. To think of not going to the mission field after all these years of searching and waiting and preparing engendered terrible inner conflict.

One morning while walking to church, Gus felt the burden was too much for him to endure. As he cried out to heaven, he heard God's voice in his heart: "Without faith it is impossible to please me, for he that comes to God must believe that God is, and that I am a rewarder of those who diligently seek me." (See Hebrews 11:6.)

"That's it," Gus responded. "I will diligently seek Him. I've been seeking healing, opportunity for service and encouragement, but not Him—Jesus."

At that moment, darkness became light, and sorrow turned to joy. From that day on, Gus was never again troubled with convulsions.

Another wonderful thing happened to Gus—he met a young lady by the name of Pauline Kohn. Pauline's parents also had come from Germany to settle in New York City. The family attended a German Baptist Church. It wasn't until she was hired by Macy's department store and met fellow-clerk Ellen Olsen, who invited her to attend Dr. Simpson's Gospel Tabernacle, that she began the journey that would eventually take her to China. It was at the Gospel Tabernacle under Dr. Simpson's ministry that she found the Lord and received a call to become a missionary. She resigned her position at Macy's and became a full-time student at Nyack.

It wasn't long until Gus and Pauline became friends. From Gus' point of view, there were several things in Pauline's favor—she was a beautiful German blond, with proper manners, not too tall for a short man like him—and she also wanted to go to China! Wishing to show Pauline how he felt about her, Gus determined to give her a ring. To his amazement, however, she declined.

"Gus," she said, "a ring will be too extravagant. You know that much of the money missionaries get for their support comes from poor, godly and sacrificially giving people who do not themselves have a diamond. In fact, many folks are putting their jewelry—rings, watches, bracelets and the like—into the offering plates at the Gospel Tabernacle so missionaries will get their full allowance. You've seen that yourself. How could we spend that money for a ring?"

Although somewhat deflated, Gus nodded his agreement.

"There is a second reason," Pauline continued. "I have heard that there are pirates, robbers and bandits in great numbers in China. A diamond could be very tempting to such men. But," she continued with a smile, "I do need a wristwatch. The robbers won't be able to see it since all my dresses have long sleeves."

Gus got the message.

"Then you shall have an engagement watch," he replied. "Each time it ticks it will remind you of my love for you."

At that time, it was the policy of the Mission Board to send missionaries to the field single. Once there, they were to wait two years to see whether one or the other would be unable to take the rigors of the climate or learn to speak the language. If such was the case, an engagement could be broken, but not a marriage.

The wedding would have to wait.

# 4

# *China at Last*

The night before Gus and Pauline left Elberta on their way to China, brother Fred read Isaiah 49 in family devotions. Then he turned to his future sister-in-law.

"Pauline," he said, "this is your chapter. Take it with you. The Lord will never forget nor forsake you. And, may many come to Him 'from the land of Sinim [China].' " He flipped back to the beginning of the chapter. "Look at the second half of verse 6: 'I will also give thee for a light to the Gentiles, that thou mayest be my salvation unto the end of the earth.' But the greatest promise is in verses 12 and 13: 'Behold, these shall come from far: and, lo, these from the north and from the west; and these from the land of Sinim. Sing, O heavens; and be joyful, O earth; and break forth into singing, O mountains: for the LORD hath comforted his people, and will have mercy upon his afflicted.' "

Though partings are always sorrowful, for Gus' mother it was especially true. It would be seven years until Gus' first furlough. Because of her age, Mother Woerner did not feel that she would see her son again on earth. Yet she asked the Lord to help her not to weep as she said good-bye. God had answered her prayers in sending Gus to the mission field and she was determined to be brave as he went. After all, in a very real sense, Gus was her overseas representative.

Pauline sailed from Vancouver, Canada, in October 1923. Gus, along with five other missionaries, followed a month later. After experiencing weeks of sea sickness and "bunk fatigue," during which time Gus read the entire Bible, he was relieved when the ship finally docked in Yokohama, Japan. The sight that lay before him was overwhelming. The great earthquake of 1923 had left the city in ruins. As the *Empress* passed the majestic Mount Fuji and steamed on to Kamakura, the site of the forty-three-foot-tall Great Bronze Buddha, Gus, for the first time, came face-to-face with the abominations of idolatry. How he longed to tell the people of the true Savior of the world, but first, he had to learn the language.

When he arrived at Wuchow, his destination for the time being, a group of missionaries, Pauline included, were there to greet him. There were warm handshakes all around, except in Gus and Pauline's case where the appropriate action was obviously an embrace and kiss. Or was it? The happy couple were about to learn their first lesson in what was appropriate in Chinese culture. One of the senior missionaries took Pauline aside.

"The Chinese never kiss or show any kind of affection in public," she explained. "It is a serious breach of etiquette." Dr. Jaffray, who also met the new missionaries, overheard the conversation and took the occasion to point out that "not only do you need to learn the language of the people, but also their customs so that no false impression or offense might be given."

Pauline was scheduled to begin her language study in Wuchow, but Gus would proceed about sixty miles farther west into the interior to Kingyuen. It had been thirty-six days since Gus had left Elberta, Alabama. He had traveled exactly halfway around the earth, first by rail to Vancouver, then on a succession of water vehicles: the majestic *Empress*, a river steamer, a motor launch and finally on a small Chinese junk poled by coolies.

With a dictionary, suggested daily schedule and a few textbooks provided by the Mission Language Committee, all Gus needed now was a teacher. The Lord provided an excellent Chinese tutor who was also a Christian. What Gus had feared would be monotonous and difficult became fascinating.

For years, Gus had been singing "To the regions beyond I must go, I must go." Now the words changed; he was at last in the regions beyond and so happy to be there that he literally immersed himself in study despite admonitions not to do so. *The sooner I learn the language*, Gus reasoned, *the sooner I can begin to communicate the gospel*. It was reason enough to work hard.

One day he overheard the servants at the house where he was living, talking about the missionaries. The maid was telling the cook: "There are only two kinds of missionaries, good or bad"—not dumb or smart, not talented or well-educated, but "good or bad." Gus began to pray earnestly, "God, make me a 'good' missionary."

The winter and early spring months had been quiet and peaceful in the Kingyuen area. But as summer approached, rumors of unrest in the northeastern part of the province reached Gus and his companions. Soon a letter from Mrs. Oldfield (with whom Pauline was studying) arrived.

"The city of Kweilin is besieged," she reported. "My husband, traveling there along with fifteen other missionaries, is trapped. Five of the group are Alliance. Please pray."

Immediately the chairman in Wuchow advised all missionaries in the area to evacuate to Liuchow. Though reluctant, they obeyed. Then more sobering news arrived, this time from

Wuchow. The Rev. Joseph R. Cunningham, a veteran missionary in Kweilin, had been hit by a supposedly stray bullet and killed instantly.

The one blessing that came out of the unrest was that Gus and Pauline were reunited in Liuchow.

"What are we going to do?" Pauline asked her husband-to-be.

"I'm afraid Liuchow might be the next to be attacked," he answered. "We must go on to Wuchow as soon as possible. Don't worry, my love. God will take care of us." Six days later they were aboard a motor launch on the way to Wuchow.

It was not long before the fears of Gus and Pauline and the other missionaries with them came to pass. Outlaws boarded the launch and demanded money, a harrowing experience for the new missionaries, but routine to the veterans. Rice money was forcibly taken several times by various groups of sectional bandits. Despite the frightening voyage, everyone arrived safely. Eventually, all the missionaries being held captive (including Dr. Jaffray) were freed.

Early each summer the Alliance missionaries in South China gathered for the annual conference, a time of inspiration and fellowship, but also the time when they received their appointments to various locations for the coming year. Gus was appointed to Kweilin and Pauline to Pinglo for further language study.

Following conference, the missionary team usually went to Hong Kong for a rest and to look after personal matters, such as purchasing supplies or taking care of health needs by having physical or dental checkups. Since Gus had been in China for only six months he did not feel he needed a vacation. However, the senior missionaries urged him, "Take these times conscientiously. This will help you build up physical strength and resistance for the days ahead." Gus complied in spite of the deep urgency he felt to "get going" to Kweilin.

The best way to get to Kweilin was on a small Chinese junk, about sixty feet long and fifteen feet wide. At Liuchow, the party transferred to one about half that length which was pulled or poled by six coolies.

The scenery along the Dragon River was magnificent. Large, exquisite pagodas rose picturesquely on the rugged but beautiful mountains. Dozens of smaller shrines and temples surrounded them. But the farther inland the group went, the smaller the villages along the riverbanks became, even with the ever-present sampan population floating alongside.

Finally, on October 27, 1924, they arrived at their respective appointments. Although the area is often called the "Switzerland of China" for its picturesque beauty, the party had, in 225 miles of travel up the Foo River, crossed the area

150 times and ascended as many rapids. Certainly it was beautiful, but rugged as well.

One of Gus' language requirements the second year was that he read and study the Gospel of Mark. This meant he had to learn all the Chinese characters (words) so that he could navigate the book without a dictionary. Every character he did not know, along with its meaning and tone, he wrote in the wide margin of his New Testament. At first the margins were black with ink, but by the time Gus reached the end of the book, the margins were hardly used at all. He followed this same course of study for the rest of the New Testament. He was also learning Chinese and Chinese customs in other ways than studying.

One day Gus was invited to a feast given by the chief magistrate of the province. The first course was steaming bird's nest soup, followed by numerous other delectables. Gus easily identified all the meat courses but one.

"What kind of meat is this?" he asked a Chinese man seated beside him.

"Ti Yang," came the reply.

Thinking that meant veal, Gus had a second helping. When he got home, he looked up the word in the dictionary. He could not find it. The next morning he told his teacher about the feast and mentioned the dish called "Ti Yang."

"Did you eat any of it?" the teacher asked.

"Yes, and I liked it," Gus replied.

Laughingly, the teacher explained, "Ti Yang is a fancy name for dog meat."

"Well," Gus responded, "it's too late to get sick now, but next time I'll make sure I understand what's being offered before eating it!"

Now after two years of study and upon completion of their fourth and fifth language examinations and called full-fledged missionaries, Gus and Pauline were looking forward to conference time when they could be married. It did not prove to be quite so uncomplicated as they had envisioned.

About that time the warlords of Kwangsi began to plan a new offensive to drive out "reddish" forces from northeast Kwangsi province. Everyone was jittery. Then came news that The Christian and Missionary Alliance was ordering all missionaries to Wuchow and then to the coast. Conference for this year (1925) was cancelled!

"What shall we do, Gus? What about our wedding?" Pauline asked.

"We'll get married on June 5 anyway," he replied reassuringly.

Since Dr. Jaffray had already left for Hong Kong and foreigners had to have an American consul present to witness such ceremonies, Gus and Pauline traveled to Canton where there was a U.S. official. They took their vows on the grounds of a hospital, with no attendants nor family members present. Nevertheless, they were conscious of the Lord's presence and, despite hasty planning and travel, all went beautifully—until it came time for the honeymoon.

Dr. Jaffray had arranged for a place for the newlyweds to stay, but for several days only a noon meal was available. The rest of the time they had to fend for themselves. A few days later, when the British boycott ended, the Woerners moved to House #22 on Cheung Chow which had been built by Dr. Jaffray. The situation was less than ideal, however, since twelve couples plus several single and married women were occupying the dwelling designed to accommodate only six couples! To make matters even worse, the ladies were all assigned to three bedrooms and the men to the other three! Such was the Woerners' initiation into married life. It was a good time to remember that being a missionary is a calling!

That fall, Gus and senior missionary W.H. Oldfield attempted to return to Wuchow by train. At noon of the first day, bandits attacked the train. All the passengers fell to the floor, some even squeezing so tightly under the seats that they later needed help to get out. But the train did not stop. Upon arriving at their destination, they found out why: The engineer had been killed and the fireman had taken his place at the throttle. When the men arrived safely in Wuchow, they were immediately urged to go back to Hong Kong to bring the others to the interior also. That was very good news for the "inmates" of House #22 on Cheung

Chow. They were by now more than eager to return to work after their enforced and prolonged "vacation."

The Woerners were told to go to Pinglo where Pauline had been the previous year and await their specific assignment. In her heart Pauline hoped they would be able to remain another year in Pinglo. With so much displacement of personnel, it would be good to stay in the same place a little longer before going to an entirely new location. Gus, on the other hand, was willing to go anywhere there were lost people. He had only one cause in mind: to get the gospel out. But his mind kept focusing on Wuchow, the location of Dr. Jaffray's headquarters. True to his commitment and heart, Gus prayed, "Lord, wherever You will. Just let me be faithful to Your calling."

# 5

# Bed Boards, Tired Feet and Robbers

As soon as they were settled in Pinglo, Pauline once again launched into the ministry she knew and loved, working with the girls at the school and doing visitation with the Bible women.

The first thing Gus did was to sit down and begin studying a map of South China, one of the five regions into which The Christian and Missionary Alliance had divided their China field. Singling out Kwangsi, the province to which they were assigned, he motioned to Pauline.

"Here's Pinglo," he said, pointing to a tiny dot near the eastern border. "But look, the province stretches about 450 miles from east to west."

"How far is it from north to south?" Pauline asked.

"Well, it looks like about 250 miles," he replied, "and we're already 250 miles northwest of Hong Kong. I would guess that the whole area is roughly 100,000 square miles."

The dozens of dots sprinkled on the map represented cities, towns and villages, all of which were as yet unreached with the gospel. *Without Christ! What a challenge that will be!* he sighed.

Pinglo was a walled city of about 80,000 people whose environs encompassed eight county seats and several hundred market towns and villages. There were two mission outstations, but what was that compared to the thousands of lost people in the vast northwest who had not heard the gospel story? The question remained: How could they be reached?

The word "colportage" is not well-known today. However, in those days, colportage was a significant and fruitful ministry method in many areas of the world, including China. Colporteurs (men and women carrying dozens of Scripture portions and tracts) traveled around the country, penetrating the remotest jungle settlements and mountain villages, distributing God's Word. Their work often took them over trails never before walked by the feet of missionaries. It was difficult and sometimes dangerous, but very rewarding. Just how rewarding it could be Gus was soon to learn firsthand.

Believing that colportage would be an effective way to penetrate this vast region, Gus contacted the agent of the British and Foreign Bible

Society in Canton, the man who had performed the marriage ceremony for him and Pauline. His response was immediate and generous.

"I will be happy for you to hire a colporteur to work under your supervision. We will even pay him," the agent said, "and I'll also supply you with all the Gospel portions you can use, free of charge. You can buy the tracts from the Alliance Press in Wuchow."

Soon Gus and his colporteur were systematically distributing materials provided by the Bible Society. They always charged just a few cents. "By asking a small fee," Gus told his assistant, "the literature will be more valuable. If we don't charge, the books and tracts will be cheapened in the eyes of the people and maybe they will just throw them away."

In each of the surrounding towns, Gus and his colporteur held an open-air service on market day. Gus played his accordion, the men sang a duet, then one of them gave a message. On one particular occasion, the colporteur quoted Jeremiah 10:3-5:

> For the customs of the people are vain: for one cutteth a tree out of the forest, the work of the hands of the workman, with the axe. They deck it with silver and with gold; they fasten it with nails and with hammers, that it move not. They are upright as the palm tree, but speak not: they must needs be borne, because they

cannot go. Be not afraid of them; for they
cannot do evil, neither also is it in them to
do good.

Then pointing to several idols standing
nearby, he said, "Those who worship idols are
more stupid than a mosquito. Even a mosquito
knows better than to try to get something from
an idol—it has no blood nor life." In one village
of about 130 inhabitants, every adult became a
baptized believer.

One day that first winter a man came to the
chapel and asked for the missionary who had
sold some books to him.

"I have read the books carefully and I want to
know if Jesus can heal my leg," he said as he
carefully pulled up his trouser leg.

Gus was shocked. From the ankle to the knee
the leg was one mass of ulcerated flesh!

"There is no doctor here, and the chapel is not
a hospital," Gus responded sadly.

"Do something anyhow!" the man begged.

Looking to the Lord for help, Gus swabbed
the leg with a solution of iodine and water and
bound it with a pillowcase. The man thanked
him and started away.

"Please wait a minute," Gus called after him. "I
want to pray that Jesus will bless what I have done
and heal your leg. I am not a doctor, but Jesus is
the great Healer as well as the Forgiver of sins."

Gus prayed and the man left. About one
month later he showed up at the mission door.

"Missionary," exclaimed the man, "Jesus healed my leg!" Once again he pulled up his trouser leg. There was not one ulcer left! The flesh was like the flesh of a child.

"Praise the Lord," breathed Gus.

It was 1925. Fourteen years earlier, China's patriarchal form of government had suddenly become a republic. But the change was too drastic, the results chaotic. Large sections of the country warred with other sections. Robbers and soldiers harassed the people. Missionaries and national Christians were threatened. Kidnapping and murder were rampant. It became almost commonplace for the missionaries to receive a call to evacuate to a more settled location, usually Hong Kong.

When the Woerners first went to China, there were many provincial wars. Now, with the new republic, Sun Yat-sen, the leader, and his right-hand man, Chiang Kai-shek, tried to forge a democratic form of government. But the Russian advisers forced them to establish a communistic style government. What leverage the Russians enjoyed resulted from the time when Great Britain refused to lend China $25 million. Russia had stepped in, providing the money. Now, however, the tables had been turned and Russia was forcing General Chiang Kai-shek to flee to Formosa (now called Taiwan). The air was filled with a political menu of communistic rhetoric. Worst of all, anti-God and anti-church beliefs were being forced on the people with increasing intensity. The future was, to say the least, uncertain.

For the Woerners, their lives became a series of running from and returning to their work in Kwangsi province. And their ministry was fraught with numerous interruptions, inconveniences and dangers of all kinds. Yet neither they nor any other missionaries considered withdrawing unless and until the doors were finally closed or they were expelled.

"Surely you can't work under these conditions," they were told. Even government officials suggested they go home. But the Woerners replied, "In spite of all the difficulties, we plan to stay. Did Jesus leave because the thorns pricked or because He was thirsty? Did Stephen run away from the stones? Or Daniel from the lions? Our God is with us and we will stay."

The opportunity for another colportage trip presented itself a couple of years later when the executive committee at the annual field conference asked Mr. Oldfield to make a trip to Poseh, the town farthest west in Kwangsi province. Perhaps Poseh could become a center from which to evangelize that as yet unreached part of northwestern Kwangsi. Because of the unstable conditions in the area, the committee asked Gus to accompany Oldfield.

The entire party consisted of the two missionaries, two Chinese pastors, one colporteur and four carriers who would handle the personal effects of the missionaries, plus 10,000 Scripture portions, calendars and tracts. Another 10,000 portions were mailed ahead to large cities along the way. Gus could hardly believe that they would all be sold.

"Oh, you'll be surprised," Oldfield replied with a smile. "We'll just literally sow the land with the gospel seed so the people who hear the message as we preach will have it in print to read later." His prediction turned out to be true. Sometimes the quantities even had to be limited at one location in order to have enough for other places farther down the road.

Protocol demanded that when the missionaries entered a city they went first to the head man, gave him a package of their materials and explained the purpose of their visit. Then, with his consent they would go into the streets. Not a single official on the entire journey refused the literature. One thanked them profusely.

"It seems you have dropped down from the skies, for no white man has ever before penetrated this district," he told the men.

Robbers caused the biggest problem on the trip. The missionaries were often cautioned not to use certain paths. One tribesman informed them that a robbery and kidnapping had occurred recently in a particular area. Shrugging his shoulders, he said, "Me no go that way." Nor did the missionaries!

The terrain was so rugged that highwaymen could easily hide at one of the frequent sharp turns in the road and pounce on their unsuspecting victims. However, along the roads and paths and in the villages were also many people who gladly listened to Gus and Mr. Oldfield and bought their literature.

One of the most difficult parts of the trip was finding a place to sleep. Sometimes the men slept on beds, bed boards or tables. And more than once they laid down to rest on coffins!

The first night that the entourage stopped at an inn, Gus was amazed to see workers taking the doors down from their hinges.

"What are they doing that for?" he whispered to his colporteur.

"Oh, those are called bed boards. When there aren't enough beds for all the travelers, the doors are taken down and used for mattresses. See, they're putting them on trestles." The man paused briefly as a slight smile crossed his face. "They aren't very soft, but at least we'll have something to lie on."

Despite not having slept well at times, the men were always happy to rise at 4:30 and wash and shave by the dim light of a peanut oil lamp. They did not have to dress—they had not undressed the night before!

During the forty-seven days of the tour, Gus and his companions walked thirty-seven days and scaled mountains up to 3,000 feet high. They often followed rocky stream beds, which in the rainy season could be very dangerous. Some days they could walk only 30 *li* (LEE—one li equals one-third of a mile), while other days they walked as many as 120 *li*, depending on the distances between towns and the opportunities for witnessing along the way. Altogether on the trip, they traveled on foot about 1,500 miles and passed through more than 100 towns and villages, including thirteen county seats, with a total population of over 200,000. They held more than eighty-five open-air services and sold over 20,000 Scripture portions, 10,000 booklets and tracts and 20,000 calendars. More than 5,000 people heard the gospel preached. Most of those who listened had never heard the name of Jesus Christ nor of His love for all mankind.

At least one important decision was made on that trip: Poseh would be an ideal location for a base from which colporteur work and other aggressive itineration could be launched. A couple was needed to establish a station there. But who? And when?

After the trip, Gus' heart, like that of Dr. A.B. Simpson before him, burned with a passion for the millions of lost souls in China. He could not be content just to stay within the confines of a city when there were so many perishing in its extended environs.

"Lost! Lost!" he kept repeating. "Pauline, if you had but seen them!" She was also captivated by the word. One question flowed into the next, until

each had been answered: "Are you planning another trek? Isn't it dangerous? You haven't told me
much, but I've heard from other missionaries."

"Yes, the hopelessness on their faces! Every
time I shut my eyes I see them—and see the
change that comes when they hear the message
of life. The desire to reach them consumes me!"

"But, Gus," Pauline responded, "what about
your job here in Pinglo and in Wuchow, teaching in the Bible school?" (The Woerners spent
part of their time in Pinglo, going to Wuchow
during the school year to teach.)

"We can arrange for someone to take my
place," came the quick reply.

"Then you have my blessing," she said. "I'll put
you in God's hands. You'll be safe there. I'll continue to work here."

In November 1928, Gus returned to Poseh.
Two days before they were scheduled to arrive,
the party stopped at a small town called Po
Hong. Since it was market day, Gus and the others anticipated good opportunities to witness
for Christ. However, a student there began to
vehemently protest their efforts by trying to prevent people from accepting literature from the
"foreign devil." Gus tried to reason with the
man, but quickly realized his efforts were in
vain. Every time Gus opened his mouth to
speak, the student drowned him out.

Things might have reached an impasse had
the missionaries not met the district magistrate

who welcomed them and asked for books even before any could be given him. The magistrate himself introduced the missionaries to the people and urged them to receive their message.

Once again, on this fifty-two-day, 750-mile trip, over 20,000 Scripture portions were sold, plus 10,000 booklets and tracts and 20,000 calendars. But there was still much land to be possessed and Gus' passion burned on.

## 6

# The Three Rs—
# Robert, Ruth and
# Raymond

In the spring of 1926, Pauline began to be plagued with a series of boils and abscesses. Since there was no medical doctor in Pinglo, Dr. Jaffray advised the Woerners to go to the Southern Baptist Hospital in Wuchow. There her condition was diagnosed as a combination of streptococcus, staphylococcus and pneumococcus infections. Added to these problems was the fact that she was expecting their first child.

Because of Pauline's condition and the rapidly eroding military situation in Kwangsi province, Dr. Jaffray urged the Woerners to go to Hong Kong for the birth. They complied. But they had no sooner arrived than Pauline fell and was rushed to the Matilda Hospital. The next morning, April 6, 1926, Robert George, their first son, was born—a month premature.

A month later, war broke out once again in Kwangsi province, making it necessary for the Woerners to postpone their return to Wuchow. Five months later they finally received word that it now seemed safe to go back to Kwangsi. However, on the return trip to Wuchow, the riverboat on which they were traveling was attacked by a band of pirates. When shots were fired, instead of stopping the ship, the captain ordered, "Full speed ahead." With the thrust of the throttle, even in their cabin and unaware of the situation, the Woerners sensed the danger. Grabbing Bobby's bassinet, Gus shoved it under the lower bunk. Then he and Pauline stretched out on the floor beside it. Meanwhile, bullets were peppering the boat. When the noise finally subsided and it seemed safe to do so, Gus reached for the baby.

"Is he all right?" asked Pauline, her voice trembling. "I'm afraid to look." When finally she did, she saw only a whimpering child, obviously frightened by the "fireworks," but thankfully unharmed.

Just then, Gus noticed that one of their suitcases still lying on the floor had a bullet hole in it. Opening it, he found a small brass souvenir plate also with a hole in it. A bullet had gone completely through the suitcase and out the other side! It was never found.

"What if the bullet had gone through one of our heads?" Gus asked, not necessarily expecting an answer. They both shuddered. God had miraculously spared their lives—and that of young Robert George.

Since he had been born prematurely, Bobby's first year was a difficult one. Because of his mother's illness, she had not been able to nurse him and it turned out to be almost impossible to get formula that agreed with him. Then, when Bobby was a year old, he fell victim to whooping cough, making him even less robust than he had been up to that point. His progress in learning to walk was slow and he was also cutting teeth. He had been sick since early March, and by May, when Dr. Jaffray and the conference committee asked Gus to accompany Oldfield on the trip to Poseh, Bobby was still coughing. Gus really didn't want to go, but he finally agreed.

As Dr. Jaffray was bidding Gus farewell, he said, "Brother Woerner, I believe as you go forth in the Lord's work, Jesus will take care of Bobby. I'll be praying for you and for your son's healing."

Pauline was brave, not wanting her husband to stay home when, as she put it, "his duty lay elsewhere." Friends also were most supportive. Gus' mother, too, responded to a letter from Gus, saying that she would pray daily for the trip. The Lord also gave her a verse for Bobby: "I have seen his ways, and will heal him" (Isaiah 57:18).

When Gus returned from the trip to Poseh, however, Bobby looked like a famine sufferer and not like the almost normal child he had left behind a month earlier.

So, when the Oldfields left for home leave, they escorted Pauline and Bobby to the Matilda Hospital in Hong Kong. The sad news there was that Bobby had tubercular peritonitis. That meant that he would need a complete change of climate. The doctor urged Pauline to take him to America. Dr. Jaffray was notified and immediately arranged an early furlough for the family. But Gus was troubled in his spirit.

"I can't get peace of mind nor rest of soul," he confided to Dr. Jaffray. "I feel that if Jesus the Great Physician cannot heal Bobby in China, He will not heal him in America either. John 14:1 says, 'Let not your heart be troubled; ye believe in God, believe also in me.' I believe!" From that moment, Gus was at peace.

As an alternate plan, it was suggested that the Woerners retreat to the cool and invigorating climate of the Filipino city of Baguio, a beautiful mountain resort more than 5,000 feet above sea level. Though in the tropics, Baguio was known as the "City of Pines." It was an ideal place for recuperation. There, within a week, Bobby's appetite had improved. At first Gus and Pauline wheeled him around in his carriage, but after several weeks he was able to walk again. From a "little bundle of skin and bones," as his mother described him, he began to fill out and get strong. Though he weighed only nineteen pounds on arrival, when they left Baguio eight weeks later, Bobby tipped the scales at thirty-one pounds! The Chinese at Wuchow called him "a little resurrection."

On February 1, 1929, God gave Gus and Pauline "another little cherub" in the person of Ruth Marion Woerner. Since Gus was teaching at the Bible school in Wuchow, he did not go to Hong Kong for the birth. Instead, a nurse from another Mission accompanied Pauline. At the news of the arrival of little Ruthie, Gus made arrangements to meet them at the coast to bring them home.

It was 1930 and time for furlough. After a trip to visit relatives both in Germany and various parts of the United States, the Woerners settled in Philadelphia. Just one hour before Gus was to leave on his spring tour, Raymond Paul was born, February 7, 1931.

"How good of the Lord," Gus said, "to let me see him for a moment, hear him cry, hold him in my arms and kiss him good-bye."

One summer morning some months later, Gus was listening to the radio while eating breakfast. "I will be with him in trouble; I will deliver him (Psalm 91:15)," the speaker quoted. The verse caught Gus' attention, and over the next few hours the words of the text kept replaying in his mind until he began to wonder if they had some special significance for him and his family. He did not have to wait long to find out.

That very afternoon, on their way to a convention center in Philadelphia to hear William Christie speak, the meaning became clear. Several members of the family were in the front seat of their car. Mother Woerner was in the back seat with Bobby, who was standing holding on to the back of the front seat. As they rounded a curve at about fifty miles per hour, the back door suddenly swung open and Bobby fell out of the car. A vehicle coming from the opposite direction was able to stop just before hitting him.

As Gus picked up his son, he felt the little boy begin to stiffen in his arms. He laid him on the back seat, drove by the convention center to drop off two of the passengers and went on to Abingdon Hospital.

Meanwhile, someone informed the usher at the meeting what had happened. He in turn told Dr. Christie, who had just started to preach. Immediately he stopped preaching and turned the service into a prayer meeting for little Bobby Woerner.

At the hospital, the doctor examined Bobby.

"He has a slight concussion and a fractured shoulder blade and collarbone," he said. "I'll wrap him with adhesive bandages. He'll be OK."

"We're supposed to be sailing soon for China. Will that have to be delayed?" Gus asked anxiously.

"No," responded the doctor. "He'll soon be fine."

When a Chinese doctor eventually removed the bandages, he found the fractured bones perfectly healed!

Gus and Pauline were just completing their first home leave after seven years on the field, awaiting their assignment for the coming year. When news of the appointment arrived, it read "Poseh or Kweilin." The Woerners were neither joyful nor disappointed at the news—just surprised, since they had been in the Bible school at Wuchow the last four years of their first term.

"Which shall it be, Gus, Poseh or Kweilin?" Pauline asked.

"Kweilin is much closer to where we've been," Gus responded as if thinking aloud, "not too far north of Wuchow and Pinglo."

"It's pretty dangerous in Kweilin, isn't it?" Pauline asked again. "But Poseh is so far away."

"Five hundred miles west of Wuchow."

"Five hundred miles!" replied Pauline, slowly repeating the phrase as its implications became clear. *How wise would it be*, she wondered, *with China now seriously threatened by the dark clouds of communism, to take three small children to the farthest inland city from Wuchow?* In fact, should they even return to China at this time? China, with its civil wars, communist insurgents, banditry and other problems, posed significant personal danger.

The following morning, during their usual family worship time after breakfast, a reference was made in prayer to the choice of Kweilin or Poseh. Suddenly, in a most vivid manner, the faces of thousands of lost souls came before Gus. Gripped with a burden for their salvation, he made a decision. Poseh it would be.

Years later, Gus wrote: "I still remember the morning at our devotions when the verse came clear and direct. 'Follow me (to Poseh) and I will make you fishers of men.' The question boiled down to this: Whom will I put first—the Lord or the children? Matthew 10:37 came to mind: 'He that loveth son or daughter more than me is not worthy of me.' If I put the Lord first, He will make me a fisher of men. That settled it."

Throughout their missionary career, the Woerners would release their precious children to the care of the Lord and others for a year and sometimes more at a time. While they had good times together at conferences and during the summers, the children never truly lived with their parents once they were of school age. Even when forced years later to return to the States and to Toccoa Falls Institute, they lived in campus dormitory rooms while their parents lived in various small apartments elsewhere on campus.

One major decision remained before the family returned to China: schooling for Bobby who was now six years old. The Alliance had no school for missionaries' children in the Far East. The options were to leave Bobby at home with relatives, to send him to a school of another Mission or to teach him at home. They decided to teach him at home using the Calvert system, a correspondence course popular with expatriate American families at that time.

Back in China, the family once again began to experience physical problems. In such a climate as that of Poseh, it was inevitable. Ruthie came down with dysentery. Since the nearest doctor was 250 miles away and the river was so low that transportation moved at a snail's pace, Gus and Pauline felt that surely the Lord would heal Ruthie right where they were. God had led them there; surely His purposes would be fulfilled.

The Sunday after Ruthie became ill, neither she nor her mother could go to church. When Gus requested prayer for his daughter, it seemed as though the entire body of believers was electrified with the urgency of the situation, especially the women of the church.

After the service concluded, two women came to the Woerners' porch, knelt on the floor in front of the French windows and prayed. As soon as they left, two others came. Like a stream, it continued all afternoon until darkness fell. In fact, for the next three days the women faithfully prayed. The Lord answered their prayers and within three weeks Ruthie was on her way to recovery.

Two years later, Bobby had "graduated" from his mother's home classroom and was attending school in Hong Kong where he lived in the Alliance hostel. When Ruthie was five, she joined her brother there. It was hard for Gus and Pauline to leave the children for a year and sometimes more, but they felt that this was what the Lord wanted them to do. From the beginning of their missionary career, they had agreed that if they had children they would send them away to school. Now it was decision time.

With little Raymond hanging on, Gus and Pauline pulled Ruthie and Bobby into their arms and assured them that they loved them and that they would be happy at school.

"You will love it," Gus said, a catch in his throat. "You will have lots of playmates and lots of fun together. It is much more interesting here than at home. Besides, we will see you at conference time and we'll go on a big vacation to Hong Kong."

"We'll remember, Father. We're part of the team, aren't we? It's our 'job' to go to school!" the children responded.

Hugging them once more, Gus and Pauline turned to leave for Poseh. They managed to hold back the tears until they got into the rickshas and signaled the coolie to go. Finally out of sight of the children, two grieving parents let the tears flow freely. Now, only Raymond was at home with his mother and father.

While Gus was teaching in Wuchow, little Raymond began to make friends with the children of the Chinese servants at the receiving home. Sometime later, although he looked perfectly healthy and remained active, the Woerners noticed that Raymond's appetite was failing. Hoping for the best and not the worst, they set out to discover what was bothering their son. They eventually discovered that Ray was eating five meals a day—two with his playmates (the Chinese ate two meals a day—in the mid-forenoon and mid-afternoon) and three with his parents. No wonder he hardly ever seemed hungry but still looked so well!

Raymond was also speaking more Chinese than English. Since the school in Hong Kong would not take children who could not speak English, Gus and Pauline knew that he would somehow have to be forced to use English. They decided not to answer him if he spoke to them in Chinese. It was a hard but necessary process. Eventually Raymond grew proficient in English as well and was ready to go to school with his brother and sister.

# 7

# *Pioneering in Poseh*

One mission field with 3 million people? That's what Dr. Jaffray saw in Kwangsi province and its capital, Poseh.

"Poseh is a great center for the evangelization of the vast unoccupied area of Kwangsi, South China," he told Gus. "This area comprises approximately 25,000 miles, with a probable population of 3 million people without any mission station save in the city of Poseh."

Yes, Poseh was strategically situated within the borders of Kwangsi, but near the border of Yunnan on the west and Kweichow on the north. It was an important commercial center, with seventeen boats traveling regularly between Nanning and Poseh. It was also a great opium center. Huge pony caravans laden with the leaves arrived in a constant stream from adjacent provinces. And Poseh was enveloped by spiritual darkness. Gus, with Walter Oldfield and others, had visited the region earlier and seen firsthand the great need for reaching its people with the message of salvation.

There were two main language groups in the northern half of Kwangsi province— Mandarin-speaking Chinese officials, students, merchants, farmers and coolies; and aborigines— peasants, boatmen and raftsmen who spoke dialects all their own. The missionaries hoped to reach both groups, but no station had thus far been established. Poseh would be the ideal location.

When the Woerners returned to China and arrived at Wuchow, they quickly unpacked, then repacked for Poseh. A river launch took them as far as Nanning and from there they transferred to a small launch up to Poseh. It took a total of twenty-five days to travel the distance, about 600 miles, the same amount of time it had taken the Woerners to travel the 6,000 miles from North America.

They settled into the home that Mr. Oldfield and Mr. Newburn had obtained for them in Poseh. It was larger than the average house, having once been used as a rice liquor warehouse. Situated on Main Street, the ground floor became a street chapel where evangelistic meetings were held each night. The upstairs level became the missionaries' quarters. On hot days the temperature rose to more than 98 degrees in the house, causing the family to wrap their heads in wet-towel turbans. The children, however, didn't seem to notice as they played in an old-fashioned, water-filled galvanized wash-tub out in the enclosed backyard.

Two years before the Woerners' arrival, the Mission had sent a national preacher to Poseh to locate there and rent a place to live. His house was about fifteen feet wide and 100 deep. The front part served as a street chapel, the two rear sections as his living quarters. With the arrival of the Woerners, there were now two chapels in Poseh.

At first Gus and Pauline opened their doors for meetings as often as every night. Gus also made the customary visits to the chief magistrate, the chief of police and the head military men. All seemed pleased that the Woerners had come to live in Poseh. By Christmas they had their first baptismal service, comprised of fifteen people who had come to the Lord during the two years the national preacher had been there.

Almost from the beginning, Gus noticed an elderly man who regularly came to the meetings, taking his seat in the same place each night. He seemed very interested and often stayed behind for further conversation.

"My name is Cheng and I want to become a Christian," he finally told Gus one night.

"Do you know what it means to follow Christ?" Gus asked him.

"Yes," the man replied. "It means to forsake my idols. I've been a devoted idol and ancestral worshiper all my life. Now I'm afraid to tear down and cast out our family altar and shrine."

"But you must," Gus assured him. "How can we help you?"

"Will you come over to my home and help me get rid of my 'holy place'?" Gus was somewhat taken aback and nervous, having never done such a thing before. But he agreed.

At the man's house, Gus read an appropriate passage from Scripture, prayed and then proceeded to remove the ancestral tablets and incense bowls. When Mr. Cheng began to help to tear down the shrine, Gus realized that he had truly received Christ into his heart. In Poseh, there was a price to be paid for turning to God from idols and serving the living and true God.

This was by no means the only time that a new convert asked Gus to rid a house of demons. Not long after this incident, two women came with a similar request. This time, eight missionaries helped to tear down the idol shrines. Gus then pasted up gospel posters in their place.

"Remember," he cautioned the women, "these posters are not to be worshiped." The women's neighbors were deeply impressed.

Mr. Cheng had a special gift for working with children. Before long he informed Gus that there were more than 100 boys and girls coming to Sunday school—a testimony to the commitment and faithfulness of this new believer.

Gus' opportunities for ministry increased daily. One day the Bible woman, Lao Pehniang ("venerable auntie"), asked him if he would bring her a pair of magnifying glasses from Hong Kong when he came back from conference. Though he tried to explain that a doctor would need to examine her eyes first, the woman insisted. So the next time he was in Hong Kong, Gus went to a dime store, tried on several pairs and purchased the ones that fit him best!

When he got back to Poseh, the first thing the old lady told him was, "Pastor, the Lord healed my eyes while you were gone and I won't need any glasses. Just as the Lord healed the blind man by spitting on the ground and making clay and putting it on his eyes and telling him to go wash in the pool of Siloam, I did the same. And God healed me. Now I can see better than I have for a long time!"

Never mind if Gus could not see out of the glasses—at least he had a pair that fit him!

Not far from the Woerner residence was the government middle school. One day the principal arrived at Gus' door.

"Would you teach me English?" he asked timidly.

"We did not come to China to teach English, but to preach the gospel," Gus responded politely.

"I know that," the man replied, "but since I am the English teacher at my school, I am especially interested in the pronunciation."

Gus thought a moment.

"Well, if you will let me read to you from the New Testament, I will be happy to teach you one hour a day."

"That is exactly what I want," the man said with a smile and a bow. And so the lessons began.

The usual procedure was for Gus to read a sentence, then have his pupil repeat it after him. One day Gus read Matthew 7:12: "Therefore all things whatsoever ye would that men should do to you, do ye even so to them: for this is the law and the prophets."

The man stopped.

"Will you please read that verse again?" he asked.

Gus repeated it, then waited for the man's response.

"This is a more profound saying than all the sayings of Confucius, our greatest and most venerated philosopher in China," he said thoughtfully.

About a month later, the teacher asked Gus if he would be willing to tell a Bible story in English to his students one night a week. Since Monday evenings were free, Gus agreed. Not wanting to take advantage of Gus' good nature, the teacher brought his students to the chapel beneath the Woerner home—a further opportunity to make the gospel known.

Gus also became friends with Mr. Wong, the Poseh postmaster. A special bond grew between them and they talked about many topics, including America. But Mr. Wong never mentioned Christianity. After two years, Gus felt he must press the claim of Christ on him.

In response, Mr. Wong stated emphatically: "I will never become a Christian!" With that, he struck the little tea table so hard that Gus feared his hand was broken. Then the man left. Deeply grieved, Gus committed himself to pray for him.

Sometime after that, Mr. Wong came to see Gus again. After asking Gus to forgive him for his rudeness, he continued: "Ever since you asked me to accept Christ and I said 'never,' I have been troubled. My ancestors were Confucianists, and I have been bound by that superstition. Now I want you to pray for me to become a Christian."

Mr. Wong was eventually immersed in baptism and gave a public testimony of his faith in the Lord Jesus Christ. He remained faithful for the rest of his life. Once again Gus was made aware of what it really costs for a person bound by false religion to come into a relationship with the God of the Bible through His Son.

Because it had earlier been decided that the Mission would not buy any more property nor build any more missionary residences or chapels in China from Mission funds, both the missionary residences at Poseh and the chapel were rented buildings. This meant that the local believers had to pay the rent plus part of the preacher's salary.

"We must look for property we can buy," the church leaders decided one day.

Although missionary allowances had been reduced because of the Depression, Gus encouraged the little group of believers to look for a house. They finally found one, but it was "haunted." For that reason, they were able to purchase it at a greatly reduced price.

The members of the congregation went to work renovating the building into a bright, clean chapel. Its crowning glory was a bell and a belfry, the result of Pauline's contact with friends back home. Its call could be heard throughout the entire city and surrounding countryside. Scores of people came to the church and many found Christ. Who could have dreamed that a church bell could become such a significant factor in winning people to the Lord?

January 23, 1934, was truly a day of rejoicing for the little church in Poseh. On that day, the final payment was made on the "haunted" house. With the help of the Woerners, God had enabled that small congregation to secure their own property—a beacon of light in isolated Kwangsi province and a memorial to Jehovah Jireh—the Lord who provides.

But Gus was still burdened by the millions of lost souls to the north and west of Poseh. In his mind he could see them beckoning him to come.

*I must go!* responded his heart.

# 8

# *A Commitment for Life—or for Death*

It is not to be expected that the treks Gus and his companions took were leisure trips. Indeed, there were many hardships and adversities along the cow-path-like trails. The trip to visit the largest of the tribes living in northwestern Kwangsi—the Heh-i—was no exception.

The Heh-i were scattered among the Chinese in a mountainous area about six days' walk to the southwest of Poseh. They were no doubt called "Heh-i" because the word literally means "black clothes," which is what they wore.

The traveling party was made up of ten people, including the carriers, as well as Al and Ray Kowalski (later called Kowles), who wanted to establish a mission among the Heh-i.

On the whole, all days were much alike in activity and routine. After walking many *li* they would come to a small town and look for a place to sleep. Often, Gus would end up renting the gloomy attic of a home which itself wasn't much more than a dismal, dark and dilapidated woodshed or barnlike structure. Bunches of unhusked corn, unthreshed rice and other grain hung or lay in piles all around on the floor. The atmosphere would grow thick with dust as the group shuffled around finding a space to lie down.

Although the travelers were exhausted from the day's journey, sleep was often slow in coming. The men could usually manage to keep the mosquitoes from biting by hanging a net over themselves. But nothing could prevent the hordes of fleas, bedbugs and other vermin from attacking the tired and defenseless human bodies which had invaded their territory.

The next morning, like clockwork, Mr. Su, the colporteur, would rise about 4:30 a.m. and rouse his assistant to build a fire, heat the water and boil the rice, while he himself prepared the vegetables. Although it was still dark, Gus and the others would breathe a prayer and arise to face the duties of the day. Reaching for the matches, they lighted the lantern, then took off the extra pair of trousers and the sweater they had worn to keep themselves warm during the cold night. All that remained was to find and put on their shoes, shave and knot their ties.

The mosquito net was always inspected for dirty cobwebs that the rats and other quadrupeds had knocked loose from the rafters during the night. Once all the undesirable intruders were banished, everything, including the extra changes of clothes that had been used as pillows, was wrapped in an oilcloth sheet in preparation for the journey and the possibility of rain. The last job before eating in the near darkness (Gus thought it was just as well that it was difficult to see!) was to treat their bruised and blistered feet.

The meal concluded, the day's journey was begun. Several miles later, the first streaks of dawn appeared, and after another hour or so, the sun rose over the crest of the mountain range. By that time, they had walked thirty *li*. Lunch was cold rice, hard-boiled eggs and anything else left over from breakfast. They had no options—there was no place along the narrow trail to buy food. Many hours later, having ascended and descended at least one mountain range under blazing sun or chilling winds, they finally arrived at their destination, somewhere around thirty miles and six hours later.

It was market day. The crowd was gathering. Gus located an inn and the men prepared a place in the attic for their bed. They felt fortunate to scare up a little straw this time as the board-and-pole floor looked terribly uneven and hard. Gus didn't bother to ask the proprietor for permission to use the straw. In a tribal village he couldn't chance a refusal, for if one inn owner refused, so would all the others.

Now it was time to prepare for the evening service. That, after all, was the reason for this long trek. Sore feet were once again washed and dressed. Next they selected a suitable place for the meeting and hung up some posters. Now all they needed was a crowd. But that was easy. Gus would simply get out his accordion and start to "pull" it, as the Chinese said. The people soon gathered to hear the singing and preaching and ask questions like "Does Jesus live in the foreign concession in Shanghai?" When everyone's questions were answered, the men would sell literature. In these ways the gospel was being planted in the hearts of the hearers.

In most places, the sharing of the gospel prompted many questions. In one market town an old grandfather with stooped back and a long white beard came to Gus' stand. After buying a set of Gospels, he wanted to purchase the booklet "Fleeing Error; Seeking Truth." However, when Gus asked three cents for it (the production cost was actually eight cents), he said he could not afford that much money and turned away disappointed.

Pitying the poor old man, Gus was going to let him have a copy for one cent.

"No," the colporteur objected. Perhaps he knew something Gus did not know.

That evening after supper, who should come to the inn where Gus was staying but the same old man, bringing three cents with him and going away happy with his purchase.

Much later, the party finally spread their oil sheet on the floor, covered it with a blanket, committed their souls to Him who never slumbers nor sleeps and turned in for as much sleep as time and creeping things allowed. This was the pattern for twenty-some days.

On this particular trip, the party passed through six district cities (county seats), walked more than 1,500 *li* and managed to get in on ("chased," as the Chinese put it) nineteen different markets. A record! By catching all those markets, they had come in contact with anywhere from 200 to several thousand representatives from almost every village hidden away in the mountain valleys surrounding these centers. They also had sold more than 5,000 Scripture portions, plus as many booklets, tracts, song sheets and calendars.

The men arrived home exhausted, and Gus somewhat crippled. His foot, which had been fractured during the war and which had caused considerable pain on the previous trip, was giving him more trouble. Fearing that the strain of daily walking would be too much, Gus had bought a horse for the trip. The Kowalski brothers also shared in the cost and took turns riding except for the last five days of the trek when Gus was unable to walk at all.

On one occasion, however, the predictable patterns of these trips took on ominous overtones. One morning, on the way home from a thirty-five-day trip to Silong, Gus was surprised and thrilled to be greeted by some children at the edge of the city. "*Ye su lai liao*" (Jesus has come!), they shouted in unison. How different from the usual "*Fan Kuei lai liao*" (the foreign devils have come!) which usually greeted them.

*Praise God*, Gus thought.

The next morning, however, the reception on the trail was quite different. Gus and his helpers had just crossed a mountain and were entering a narrow ravine when suddenly they heard a gun-shot!

"Don't move!" shouted a man from across the valley as he slowly advanced, revolver in hand. Gus turned his head and looked in front of him. Another gunman! He looked behind. Another gunman! There was no way to escape.

"Who are you? What are you doing here? Do you have any opium?" asked the head robber as he approached Gus.

"We're from the Jesus Chapel in Poseh," Gus replied.

"Search the baggage!" ordered the robber.

After inspecting every basket and finding no opium, the robbers began to frisk each man. Grabbing Gus' pen, one of them asked, "A pen? Is it a good one?"

"It is a good one, but it leaks," Gus responded, showing the man a spot of ink on his finger. At that, the robber handed it back. Then he caught sight of Gus' compass, shook it and held it to his ear.

"A watch?" he asked. Since it did not tick, he handed it back.

Picking up Gus' camera, flashlight and a pair of binoculars, the robber leader asked for $100 "rice money." Gus and his friends managed to scrape up $85. Accepting it "with thanks," the bandits disappeared into the distance.

Most feared by the missionaries, however, was the possibility of being kidnapped. A relatively common occurrence, usually one or two travelers could be carried off at a time. But sometimes four or more unwary ones would find themselves imprisoned in a small hut or cave in the mountains, to be kept there until a sizable ransom was forthcoming.

In 1925, for example, bandits seized a group of Chinese travelers, including four Christian leaders. To prevent any attempt at freedom, the bandits chained them together in groups of three or four. The four Christians had chains placed around their necks and fetters round their ankles, with only about a foot of chain between them. When one moved, all were forced to move. When one got up, all had to rise. Although there was much quarreling and cursing among the other prisoners, the four believers managed to maintain a spirit of love for each other.

Meanwhile, Dr. Jaffray heard of their captivity and wrote to Mr. Oldfield in Hong Kong to come to him in Wuchow. Gus was chosen to accompany him. Since it was so dangerous to travel between Hong Kong and Canton, the men were given the privilege of refusing. However, Oldfield and Gus both accepted the responsibility. They decided that traveling by land presented fewer potential difficulties than traveling by boat, so Gus purchased tickets and they boarded the train.

The journey to the Chinese border passed without incident, but once at the border it seemed that all hell broke loose. First there was a fusillade of bullets pouring in and over the train cars. The passengers scrambled to the floor. Three were hit by bullets. Once the train stopped, the robbers came down the aisles. They searched Mr. Oldfield, then made him help them search Gus and his baggage. Eventually they released them both to go on to Canton. There they boarded a steamer bound for Wuchow.

At Wuchow, they found Dr. Jaffray poring over a letter stating that, since their first two notes had been ignored, if the robbers did not receive the demanded ransom within seven days, the heads of the four believers would be forwarded to Dr. Jaffray.

Was it only a ploy to get the money or would there be four martyrs? The men prayed for wisdom in handling the situation.

During this time, a little church near where the men were interned asked for prayer for the four men. Someone in the crowd approached the leader and asked the name of the robber chief.

"Why, I know that man," he said. "I met him when I was a robber. I'm no longer one, but when I was, I saved that man's life. If I ask him, he'll release those four men."

And so it was that, although the men were ragged, filled with vermin and without a bath the whole time, all four of them were released—156 days after being captured!

For Gus and his fellow workers, "to the regions beyond" was a commitment for life—or for death.

# 9

# *A Tale of Three Cities*

Although there were many large cities in China, as well as thousands of smaller hamlets and villages, most of Gus and Pauline's work was centered in or originated from three large cities. One city, Poseh, became the focal point of many treks into the far west and north of South China, while in the other two cities—Liuchow and Wuchow—the Woerners taught. It was also in Poseh that their friendship with Dr. Jaffray blossomed into deep-seated and mutual respect that would later inextricably entwine their lives. These, then, are the cities of Poseh, Liuchow and Wuchow.

# *Poseh*

"I don't want you to go," cried Bobby with tears streaming down his cheeks. "Daddy, don't leave us. Stay here in Poseh with us."

Gus was about to make another foray into his mission field of 3 million people. Although little Bobby did not know that the section of Kwangsi province his father planned to visit included some of the most inaccessible, unprotected and neglected areas of the entire area, his parents were only too conscious of the dangers involved. They knew that the Sino-Japanese War being fought in Manchuria and Shanghai could easily escalate into a global conflagration. Besides, a strong anti-French (and therefore antiforeigner) feeling was increasing the tension at Poseh. It was time for Gus to explore the regions beyond his immediate environment.

"Pauline," Gus said one day, "to leave you and the children at this time would seem the height of folly, if . . . "

"Yes, Gus, but I know . . . "

"What else can I do? I keep hearing the verse, Ecclesiastes 11:4: 'He that observeth the wind shall not sow; and he that regardeth the clouds shall not reap.' It keeps coming with increasing force. I must answer the call."

"And God will bring you safely home, dear. Go with His blessing and mine too," Pauline answered. She wiped away a tear, but Gus did not see it.

"Don't cry, Bobby," she whispered, cuddling her son to her side. "Daddy has to go. We want him to tell more people about Jesus so someday everyone will know. You want him to, don't you?"

Bobby's head nodded slightly.

With the memory of the farewell etched in his mind, Gus began a journey of over 300 miles, mostly on foot. He and his companions—eight carriers, Mr. Yuen (the Poseh evangelist) and Harry Lang, the missionary from Kweiping— would enter the remote mountain areas northeast of Poseh, passing through country which for years had been the rendezvous for remnants of the defeated communist army. These lawless hordes had been responsible for untold suffering, including the massacre of 10,000 people in the area.

Because of bandit activity, the only condition under which the authorities permitted the group to travel was to follow a heavily guarded caravan. The one about to leave Poseh consisted of 2,000 pack horses, over 1,000 coolies and an entire regiment of soldiers, followed by a large group of "parasites" including Gus' party.

Days were spent marching dusty roads with little or no food to buy and crowded sleeping quarters, especially if the men were late arriving at the stopping point. One such night was spent in the dirty loft of an old stable. It was so bad that the missionary party got up shortly after midnight, ate their rice and started off at about 3 a.m. to try to find better accommodations for the following night. Now they were on their own, without the protection of numbers and military authority.

The "motel" that night turned out to be the attic of a salt factory. Twenty-four hours a day a low fire smoldered under eight huge vats of yellowish brine being boiled down to salt. After two nights there, the men's eyes began to burn from the fumes and their clothes smelled like smoked Virginia ham.

"As ye walk, preach." This is the Mandarin rendering of the phrase, "As ye go, preach." This was exactly what Gus and his companions did while following the caravan—used their time persuading their fellow travelers to purchase Scripture portions.

One day Gus caught up with a Chinese gentleman who was carrying a copy of the Gospel of Mark.

"Pastor," the man asked, "do you have the other four books in the series? I would like the complete set." There were many such opportunities to witness along the road during the day and in the camps at night.

May 5 dawned clear and seemingly peaceful. In fact, in this rugged terrain with its narrow, often slippery paths, swift swollen streams and numerous unprotected areas, Gus and his companions recognized that at any moment they could be stopped, robbed and perhaps even kidnapped by bandits who roamed the countryside. With a young family waiting for him back in Poseh, such concerns weighed heavily on Gus' mind. Today was no different.

Suddenly, in Chinese, the Lord spoke to him: "Fear not, for I am with thee" (Genesis 26:24). What comfort these words brought! But, at that moment, he did not know that the Holy Spirit was fortifying him for what lay ahead that very day.

After stopping in a village long enough to distribute tracts and to hold a short service, the men continued on their way. The group had just traversed a mountain pass and were entering a two-necked, bottle-shaped valley, when suddenly from the opposite side, halfway up the mountain, someone shouted, "Who are you? What is your business? What official authority have you?"

"We are booksellers out on a preaching tour and we're on our way home," Gus responded as they continued to walk toward the voice.

Suddenly, a shot rang out. Gus shouted to the carriers to "not walk." Everyone stopped, except the guide. He ran away at full speed. At that, the bandits fired three more shots. The entire group managed to crouch behind the rocks and boulders except Mr. Lang and Gus, who at least removed his white pith helmet so he wouldn't be so obvious a target.

The attack had been carefully planned. Within moments, armed men surrounded the travelers. A spokesman approached Gus.

"You are an opium caravan, are you not?" he asked, fingering the trigger of the revolver in his hand.

"No, only booksellers." The bandits apparently did not believe they were telling the truth and began to search every bag, basket and bundle. Eventually they were satisfied that the group carried no opium.

The leader came back to Gus.

"Lao Pan (literally 'old board,' meaning boss or manager), if we had found opium in your possessions, we would have confiscated everything you have and imprisoned you. However, we want some 'food money' and then we will let you go."

Gus produced 25 French dollars.

"What!" the man roared, "I want $50 at the very least."

Gus had $50 hidden away in a shabby basket. He was tempted to say he had no more, but his conscience got the better of him.

"I have a little more in a basket," he said finally.

Gus hoped the man wouldn't follow him to the basket so he could save some of the money for the remainder of their trip home. But the bandit watched his every move with eagle eye. When he saw the roll of bills, he snatched it away.

"Is that all you have?" he asked sharply.

"Yes," replied Gus, "but could you leave us enough to get home?"

Instead of offering to return some of the money, the bandit asked for the "loan" of Gus' and Mr. Lang's flashlights. After about an hour, which seemed more like two or three, the bandits said, "Gather up your things and go. No one will harm you."

It did not take long for the party to leave. Before they did so, however, they left the bandit spokesman a set of Gospels, some books and tracts, a calendar and a hymnbook. *Perhaps*, thought Gus, *someday some of these things will cause these men to turn to Christ*. The guide who ran away was never heard from again.

Thankful and praising God, the little group was welcomed home some days later. There would be more treks in Kwangsi province in the future, and more dangers, but also more sowing of the seed.

Up to this time Gus and his companions had faced bandits, uncooperative soldiers and many other problems. But on a following trip, another kind of danger confronted them.

At this time, Al and Ray Kowalski were living with the Woerners in order to learn the Mandarin language. When Gus left on an extensive itinerating and bookselling trip to the west and north of Poseh, they asked to go with him. Gus agreed.

Remembering the problems he had had with his leg on a former trip, Gus again decided to buy a pony-sized horse just in case he would need it. It would be needed—but not in the way Gus expected.

The second morning, when the men were in an area occupied by the Lolo tribe, Al suddenly became violently ill. Gus thought it might be ptomaine poisoning, but the local Christians felt the Lolos had poisoned the missionaries' water. Despite the prayers of many, Al did not improve.

"Please read to me from the Bible," he begged Ray.

"What book?" Ray asked.

"Mark."

"What chapter?"

"Sixteen."

When Ray got down to verse 18, "If they drink any deadly thing, it shall not hurt them; they shall lay hands on the sick, and they shall recover," Al sat up.

"That's it," he said. Gus and the others laid hands on him and called on the Great Physician to have mercy on him and on the Lolo people. The next morning Al was much better—and he had a horse to ride. A few weeks later, thirty-one new believers were baptized, the single largest number during the Woerners' years in Poseh.

Scenes from those treks would remain indelibly impressed on Gus' mind for years to come: acres of once-cultivated fields lying in waste; crumbling, dilapidated walls marking the sites of once prosperous towns; on the mountains, in valleys, ravines, caves and temples, among dark ruins of villages and along the roadsides, skulls and skeletons of decimated humanity—testimony to the cruelty of men. But, in it all, Gus and his colleagues had found hundreds eager to hear the gospel message.

This then was the Woerners' ministry in Poseh: living and working in the city, but undertaking two long treks and many shorter ones each year to reach the numerous tribes of Chinese and aborigines in the province.

## *Liuchow*

"Pauline," Gus called to his wife from the front door, letter in hand.

"Is it good news or bad?" Pauline asked, wiping her hands on her apron.

"Well, you can decide. How would you like to go to Liuchow for a month? We could go on to conference from there."

"Why go a month early?" Pauline wondered.

"You know, there's a short-term Bible school each May in Liuchow. I'm being asked to teach there this year."

The goals of these annual sessions were to help ministry-oriented young men increase their Bible knowledge and qualify for study at the regular Bible school. Many became better witnesses and helpers in the church or as

missionary assistants on bookselling trips or doing full-time colportage work as a result of these
classes. The Woerners decided that it would be a
good use of their time to accept the invitation to
participate.

While Gus taught his classes, Pauline taught
singing, that is, she taught the young people and
children Western hymn tunes by singing them
over and over until they could remember them
on their own. Because of their tonal language,
the older Chinese could not learn the English
tunes, but the children and young people loved
Western songs.

One night one of the students in Gus' class
laughingly testified, "Studying the Bible is like
eating dried duck. The more you chew it, the
better it tastes." The Woerners prayed that God
would use them to help these students understand the beauties and mysteries of the Bible
and equip them to expound the truth to others.

Once classes were over, the Woerners went
on to Wuchow for conference and then to Hong
Kong, with Ruth and Ray in tow. Bobby had already been in school there for a year, living in
the Alliance hostel. It was great to be together
again as a family, even for a short time.

## Wuchow

At conference one year later the Woerners
were assigned to Wuchow to help fill in the gap
left when two Chinese teachers became ill.

Wuchow was the headquarter city for The Christian and Missionary Alliance in South China. At that time Dr. Robert Jaffray was the field director. Although Gus had met Dr. Jaffray when he applied for missionary service and had worked under him since coming to China, the two men now developed a close friendship that would last over many years.

Just before leaving Hong Kong to join Gus who had gone ahead of her to the conference, Pauline was suddenly stricken with a high fever. Her illness turned out to be a combination of malaria and flu, causing a series of severe chills and fever.

One day, alone in the hostel and burning with fever, she begged the Lord for deliverance. Suddenly, she seemed to hear a chorus of voices singing "The Doxology." She began singing too and immediately broke out in heavy perspiration. The fever abated. The crisis was over. Pauline would never forget this special gift of healing from the Lord.

However, she was not completely well. In fact, she continued to suffer for the next two years and was unable to attend the field conferences. During those months she suffered a slight hemorrhage which at first caused great concern, but, in answer to prayer, had suddenly stopped.

About six months later a letter came from a lady in Warren, Pennsylvania, in whose home Gus had visited while on missionary tour.

"What is the problem?" she asked. "While I was ironing one day, a great burden of prayer came to me for you. I left my ironing board and called on the Lord to undertake for you and for whatever the problem was. After the burden lifted, I went back to my ironing. What was wrong?"

When the Woerners checked the dates on the calendar, they realized that that was the day the hemorrhaging had stopped. Certainly this could truly be called divine healing—with the intercessor 10,000 miles away!

By late November the regular teachers were able to resume their duties at Wuchow, so the Woerners returned to Poseh. What a joy it was to be home again!

But not for long.

# 10

# *To the Wild Men of Borneo*

For most ordinary individuals the responsibilities of chairman of the vast regions of Kwangsi, South China, would have been more than a full-time challenge. But Dr. Jaffray was no ordinary man. He began looking east to the Netherland East Indies (Indonesia) with its vast population. He became increasingly determined to broaden the missionary effort there.

One morning in 1927 Gus entered Jaffray's office. He found him poring over scrawled notes, maps and sailing schedules.

"Gus," he began without the usual preliminary small talk, "I'm going to 'sound out' the South Sea Islands. I plan to sail soon."

"But, Dr. Jaffray, how will you get there?"

"Oh, God will take care of that," Jaffray responded with a twinkle in his eye.

"You mean you want to go to the wild men of Borneo? They're headhunters and cannibals!" Gus sputtered.

Dr. Jaffray chuckled.

"We'll tame them with the gospel," he responded. "Besides, there are many other tribes there. I'm on my way."

In January of 1928, Jaffray sailed from Hong Kong south toward the islands of British Borneo. At the first stop, he haunted the docks searching for a steamer heading to Dutch Borneo. Three days later a Dutch oil tanker pulled into port.

"I'd like to get on that boat sailing to Balik-papan," he told the man in the ticket cage, nodding in the general direction of the tanker.

"No," the agent replied gruffly. "This is not a passenger ship." But Dr. Jaffray was not to be discouraged. Undaunted, he went directly to the captain of the ship, a Dutchman who, thankfully, spoke English.

"I would like to accompany you to Dutch Borneo," Jaffray told the man. The answer was the same—no! The tanker, he said, was expressly forbidden by law to take passengers. Anyway, there was no vacant cabin.

"I don't need a cabin. I just need to get to Balik-papan," Jaffray persisted. "Could you give me standing room?"

Swayed by the persistence of this North American, the captain thought a moment, then finally capitulated.

"We'll do better than that," he promised. "We'll put a cot on the deck. And, to satisfy the law, we'll make you the Fourth Officer!"

"What will my duties be?"

"If the first three die, you take charge!"

In Dutch Borneo, Jaffray encountered numerous tribes, including the storied Dyaks in whom he was most interested. They were river people. Even young children could paddle their famous canoes down the watery highways. Their houses were built of bark and on stilts. The river was obviously central to the Dyaks' daily life. Clothes were washed in the river and pounded clean on the large rocks that lined it. The Dyaks also bathed in the river—then took the water home for cooking and drinking!

In all his trekking among the Dyaks, Jaffray found only one man who was a Christian. Deeply moved by their lost condition, Jaffray's heart heaved in rhythm with the great heart of the God of heaven who had sent His Son to die for these people. This kingdom of Satan had never been confronted. The powers of darkness had not been pushed back. Jaffray determined that the Prince of Darkness should be—and would be—challenged soon.

After his return to China, Jaffray felt God's leading to organize what he called the China

Foreign Missionary Union (CFMU). He applied to the Alliance headquarters in New York for funds, but was advised that none were available. Perhaps it was not the time to establish such an entity.

However, one night Jaffray had a dream, a dream which distressed him greatly. In the dream he saw blood spots on his hands. They were there because he had not proceeded with plans to enter Indonesia. He realized then and there that God wanted him to pursue his vision. The Lord would make a way for him. And, indeed, the record shows that, as the years went by, the Dyaks, the so-called "wild men of Borneo," under the preaching of the gospel, became loving and lovable people who contributed amazingly to the evangelization of their own land and the bringing of thousands to the feet of Christ. (See *Weak Thing' in Moni Land*, by William A. Cutts; *No Sacrifice too Great*, by Ruth Presswood Hutchins; *A White Lady Doing Nothing in the Tropics*, by Mary Dixon, earlier volumes in The Jaffray Series of Missionary Portraits.)

Finally, Jaffray's plans were approved and the Chinese Foreign Missionary Union came into being. At that time, more than 5 million Chinese, many of them prosperous merchants, were living on the South Sea Islands. The formation of the society, Jaffray felt, would not only draw North American missionaries to work there, but wealthy Chinese and other Chinese Christians would also

support and serve as missionaries to their own
people living in the area. Although history shows
that not all the goals and aims of the society were
realized, the CFMU served as an impetus to
launch the work.

In 1928 the first five missionary appointees
were sent from America. Gus was asked to meet
them upon their arrival in Hong Kong, help
them transfer to the first ship going to
Indochina and accompany them to Saigon to
meet with Dr. Jaffray who had preceded them
there.

By the time the party (including the Brills, the
Fisks and David Clench) arrived in Saigon, Gus
had shared with them Dr. Jaffray's burden and
dream for this exciting new outreach. At the end
of the Indochina field conference, already in
session when they arrived, Gus saw Dr. Jaffray
and the new contingent off for Java and then returned home.

The Woerners returned from furlough in
1931. They were no sooner settled once again in
Poseh when a letter arrived from Jaffray stating
that Gus and Pauline would be a great help to
him in the development of the new field. Would
they consider coming?

It was a difficult decision. As much as the
Woerners loved Dr. Jaffray, they felt they had to
tell him that the thought of leaving Kwangsi had
never entered their minds, especially since they
were still in the process of establishing Poseh as

a center of outreach to the whole area. The Woerners settled into the work, concentrating this time on the Hsein Cities, the county seats of the vast northwestern quarter of Kwangsi province.

Three years later word once again arrived from Dr. Jaffray, this time accompanied by an official invitation from the Indonesia conference for the Woerners to transfer to Borneo.

As they were giving the request serious thought, Gus had a dream. He was in an army and had received orders to go to the front. The seriousness of the order greatly distressed him and he began to cry. Then the scene changed. He appeared to be walking with Dr. Jaffray on the large veranda of the receiving home in Wuchow. Dr. Jaffray asked him why he was crying. When Gus told him, Jaffray said tenderly, "Brother Woerner, don't weep. The Lord will go with you and all will be well in the end."

The meaning of the dream seemed clear to Gus: He and Pauline should proceed at once to Indonesia.

They said nothing to anyone until official word of the change was announced at conference time. In the meantime, they taught in the Bible school at Wuchow while the Kowles brothers went to Poseh.

The move to Indonesia meant adjusting to a different part of the world, learning a new language (fortunately the new one would not be tonal), leaving their little home in Poseh and basically starting their missionary service over again. In addition, they would be separated from their children by 2,000 miles instead of the current 200-500 miles.

"But," said Gus, "if that is what going to the 'front' means, we dare not shrink back from any danger, difficulty or sacrifice, but endure hardness as good soldiers of Jesus Christ."

Following conference, Pauline, Gus and Raymond spent a delightful vacation together with Robert and Ruth in Hong Kong. Within a few months, Raymond would join his brother and sister at the school. Partings were always difficult. Leaving China and the many friends in Poseh and Wuchow was at least as hard as saying good-bye in America after furlough. But most difficult was the fact that all their children would be away from home. They would proceed to Indonesia childless.

A special service held by their Chinese brethren recognized and confirmed the Woerners' call to Indonesia as from the Lord. While being willing to let Gus and Pauline go, the Chinese pled with them not to forget China and her great need. They also pointed out that Gus' Chinese name, Chi-hua, means "Helping China." Gus and Pauline were urged especially to assist the Chinese brethren in the CFMU.

On the boat, a woman asked what the Woerners were planning to do in Indonesia. When she heard that they were going to do missionary work, she replied, "In that case, you will have your hands full, for the place certainly is as wicked as any part of the world can be. These degenerate heathen are not worth saving!"

The Woerners looked at each other. What kind of place was this they were going to anyway? Would anything be accomplished for God's kingdom? Would they be safe there? What about their children?

July 28, 1936, the Woerners arrived at Makassar (now Ujung Pandang). Gus was immediately appointed principal of the Bible school. Although half of his thirteen years in China had been spent teaching, Gus would find that it is one thing to teach and a far different one to be principal. He also had a new language to learn. Wisely, he decided to share his duties with a Chinese teacher and the two alternated as principal and assistant. This proved to be a very satisfactory solution to what might otherwise have been an insurmountable problem.

The Bible school had been in existence for six years and this would be the first year there would be a graduating class. The program was unique. For two years the students studied at the school. That was followed by two years of practical work, then two more years of formal study—making a total of six years.

The freshman class that year was an interesting multinational group of students. Mr. Sinto, a Dyak from Borneo, had heard about the school from friends. Instead of writing for an application, he wrote simply: "God wants me to prepare for the ministry. I am like an arrow that has already been placed into the blowgun and is ready to be shot forth. I am convinced that your school is God's Bible school and I am on my way."

Since a reply was impossible, Gus simply accepted Mr. Sinto when he arrived. The Dyak proved to be a most eager student.

Then there was J. Ramboeng, a Toradja tribesman of the north central part of Celebes (now Sulawesi). Gus could not accept him because he was not a believer! Having been in the Dutch forces, he was in need of a job and decided to see if he could enroll. Finally, Gus reluctantly accepted him as a day student, assuming that he would soon tire of the discipline. But not Ramboeng. One Sunday night he accepted Christ as His Savior. He begged to be allowed to move into the dormitory, but he had no money. A friend offered to pay half the cost, so Gus found a place for him.

An old German proverb says, "All good things come in threes." The third person of Gus' trio was J. Tambayong. From the northern tip of the Island of Celebes, he had been converted after reading the first copy of *Kalam Hidup*, the Alliance Malay Bible Magazine. In the next five years, without remuneration, Tambayong secured more than 100 subscriptions to the magazine. He wanted to come to school, but he did not have the $20 to pay his fare to Makassar. So he resigned his position, found a buyer for the few small patches of garden he had and bought a ticket for Makassar. En route, he sold seven more subscriptions. Tambayong did well in his studies and astonished everyone on Easter Sunday by the creative and masterful way in which he trained and conducted a male octet in special music for the service. Such were the promising young men whom Gus had the privilege of teaching.

The Chinese Foreign Missionary Union had been formed with Leland Wang as chairman, Dr. Jaffray as vice-chairman and treasurer, and Rev. L.T. Chao and Rev. Gustave Woerner as members of the society. From this small beginning, less than ten years later the Union grew to a force of twenty-one missionaries. During that period more than 3,000 Chinese were won to Christ and innumerable blessings followed. In only a decade, for example, missionaries and national workers were able to open stations on every major island of the archipelago, build a Bible school that drew a student body of 300, baptize over 10,000 new believers and bring the gospel to major geographical areas where the name of Christ had never before been heard.*

From the inauspicious beginnings of "scrawled notes, maps and sailing schedules" and "blood spots on his hands," Jaffray and the Woerners were witnesses to the birth of a

Church that remains strong and vigorous to this
day.

* According to Dr. Peter Nanfelt in *To All Peoples*, pages 297
and 298.

# 11

# *Visitors—
and Visitors*

During their first year in Makassar, the Woerners often became the representatives of Dr. Jaffray in welcoming visitors to the school. Among those they entertained were several prominent Chinese evangelists, among them Leland Wang and John Song, who came to preach to the student body.

Dr. R.A. Forrest from the Toccoa Falls Bible Institute also came to visit some of his former students-turned-missionaries. Gus was elated to meet Dr. Forrest, the man to whom he had sent his bicycle money twenty-three years earlier. Dr. Forrest spoke to the students through an interpreter whom he jokingly called an "interrupter."

Before Dr. Forrest could leave for the States, the Dollar Steamship Line went on strike. The company called it an "act of God"; Forrest called it an "act of the devil!" because it left him stranded and without extra money to purchase a ticket on another line. Gus was able to lend him $300 which he had just received from the government as a World War I veteran's bonus. At the time Gus had no idea that within only eight years he would join Dr. Forrest at Toccoa Falls Institute (now Toccoa Falls College).

One of the most unusual guests during those days was Laeng, one of the so-called "wild men of Borneo." Just a few weeks earlier he had been chosen to be his village's human sacrifice to ensure a bountiful rice crop. As was the custom, he was dedicated to the grain god and placed in a crude shelter with only a little basket of hulled rice at his side but no water. He could eat the uncooked rice kernels until harvest time or until he died—whichever came first. Laeng felt that his being chosen for death was an honor, a responsibility he gladly acccpted.

However, in God's sovereign plan, missionary George Fisk visited the village at the time of the sacrifice.

"Can we become Christians and still offer up human sacrifices?" one of the villagers asked him.

Fisk was horrified.

"No!" he replied unequivocally. "But if you release Laeng and he lives, God will forgive you and accept you." Shortly thereafter Laeng arrived at Makassar.

All went well until two months before graduation. One day Laeng came to Gus and said he wanted to go back to Borneo. Gus tried to talk him into staying and completing his schooling, but his pleading fell on deaf ears. Realizing that this was a test of Laeng's faith and loyalty to Christ, Gus finally told him, "Say, 'Puji Tuhan' (Praise the Lord)."

Laeng refused to say it. He also refused to pray. Although Laeng had committed himself to Christ, when he was offered as a sacrifice to the rice god, the demons had taken control of him. Now, threatened by his dedication to Christ, the demons wanted him back.

"Laeng, you were rescued at the point of death. You belong to God. You are about to graduate and become a full-fledged servant of the Lord. Don't you see? The evil spirits are determined to stop that. Just say, 'Puji Tuhan.' "

But he would not.

Gus invited Laeng to stay for dinner. But he refused the invitation and left. Exhausted, Gus fell on his bed and slept. Sometime later when he awoke, he went out on the porch. A note from Laeng was waiting for him there.

"Mr. Woerner," it read, "after I left you, thinking of what you said about my belonging to Satan because I was dedicated to him, I began to understand this conflict and cried to Jesus with all my soul to deliver me from Satan's power. Instantly, involuntarily, I caught myself saying, 'Puji Tuhan!' Great peace and joy filled me. It was so real!

When I came back you were sleeping, so I am leaving this note. Jesus is victorious in my life! Puji Tuhan!" Laeng's unwelcome "visitor" from Satan had been defeated.

Years later, Laeng was elected president of the Indonesian National Preachers' Conference. Puji Tuhan!

Satan's next intended victim in the battle for Indonesia was Dr. Jaffray himself. Shortly after the Woerners arrived in Makassar, the Bible school closed for the summer vacation. Dr. Jaffray felt that a personal visit into the territory of the Boegis tribe was necessary in order to understand more fully how to reach them with the gospel. Three lady teachers, along with the Woerners, asked to accompany him. They rented a chauffeur-driven van for the trip.

"Lord, direct us and protect us," Jaffray prayed before they left. "I claim Your promise that 'everywhere your feet shall tread, I will give unto you.'"

The peninsula up which they traveled lay to the southwest of the island of Celebes (now Sulawesi). On the west side lived the Makassarese tribe; to the east, the Boegis (now Bugis) tribe. As the party traveled, small and large settlements of the Boegis began to appear along the road. Most families lived in stilted, plank houses about three meters off the ground. Some of the very poor had thatched walls. Roofs were corrugated iron. In the rice fields surrounding their huts, family groups worked together.

Late in the day the party arrived at a settlement that boasted a Chinese inn, a good place to stay for the night. The missionary men decided to try to evangelize the town, but the Boegis proved hostile to the gospel and few would accept the tracts they were offered. Those who did, after seeing the words "Indjil" (gospel) or "Isa" (Jesus) tore them up, spit on the pieces and trampled them into the dirt.

The third night of the trip Dr. Jaffray was very weary and retired early. Some hours later, just as the Woerners fell asleep, they were awakened by an outlandish scream coming from Dr. Jaffray's bedroom next door.

Pauline sat up in bed.

"Gus, get up," she cried. "Something is the matter with Dr. Jaffray."

By the time Gus put on his dressing gown, all was silent.

"Perhaps it was just a nightmare," he thought aloud. Presently he heard the shutters closing and concluded that all must be well in the adjoining room.

The next morning when they greeted Dr. Jaffray, his first words were, "My, I had an awful night." At the breakfast table he proceeded to tell them what had happened.

"I had been resting comfortably for about two hours. Then I had a vision or dream and saw a being coming toward me, the like of which I have never seen before. His face was flashing devilish hatred and rebellion against God and me, and he seemed bent on destroying me. Just one look struck terror into my soul!"

"What did you do?" Gus interrupted.

"I let out an awful yell, pulled up both my feet and kicked him out of the mosquito net! Then I awoke."

Jaffray paused to catch a breath.

"Before we started on this trip," he continued, "I was translating the book of Daniel into the Malay language. Where chapter 10 speaks of 'the prince of the kingdom of Persia,' it seems to me that God was not speaking of an actual Persian king, but rather of a spiritual being with great spiritual power given to him by Satan. Now, if that is so, can it be that every kingdom or nation has such a prince? If so, I have been attacked by a spiritual being none other than the prince of the Boegis tribe, a wicked being under the authority of Satan himself."

*Does that mean*, Gus wondered, *that every nation has such a satanic prince over it whom missionaries must take into account in their strategy for pioneer advancement?* That was something Gus would ponder for the duration of the return trip to Makassar.

That night, the group arrived home safely. However, a few mornings later Dr. Jaffray awoke not feeling well. Despite bed rest and a light diet, he continued to run a fever. Though he was not getting better, even after three days Jaffray did not want a doctor. Gus acted as his nurse. One day, as Gus was making him a cup of

"This is a *training* institute, with emphasis on training," the registrar told Gus when he enrolled at the Missionary Training Institute in Nyack in 1923. It turned out to be training in more than missions, theology and evangelism. Gus, front row right, and his buddies apparently excelled in dishwashing as well!

Pauline (Kohn) Woerner found the Lord and received the missionary call under Dr. Simpson's ministry. She resigned her position at Macy's and became a full-time student at Nyack.

Although Gus had a long-standing desire to enter the Missionary Training Institute, his plans were delayed when he was conscripted into the army. After one year, the war ended, but Gus' funds were insufficient. Finally, at 24 years of age, Gus enrolled at Nyack.

These portraits were taken as Gus and Pauline prepared to sail for China. It was the policy of the Mission Board to send missionaries to the field single. They were not allowed to marry before completing two years on the field.

Gus and Pauline were married on June 5, 1925, on the grounds of a hospital, with no attendants nor family members present. Their honeymoon was spent with twelve couples plus several single women in a house designed to sleep six couples. Men were assigned to one bedroom, women to another!

The Woerner family, L to R; Raymond, 6 months; Pauline, Robert, 5; Ruth, 2 1/2 and Gus; taken in Wuchow, Kwangsi, in 1931. Wuchow was the hub of the Alliance work in South China and Dr. Jaffray's headquarters. It was there that Gus and Pauline taught in the Bible school. A deep bond of mutual love and respect developed between Gus and Dr. Jaffray.

Gus was asked to teach at the Bible school in Liuchow. One of his students noted, "Studying the Bible is like eating dried duck. The more you chew it, the better it tastes." This picture was taken in May, 1934 at the Bible school, with Raymund and Ruth.

The city of Poseh became the hub out of which Gus and various others made long-distant treks into outlying tribal areas to hold services and distribute literature. It was dangerous, robber-infested territory, and their party was ambushed on more than one occasion. This picture shows the courtyard of the Woerner home in Poseh.
L to R: Robert, Ruth, Pauline and Raymond.

A former haunted house, this chapel was dedicated on December 2, 1934. The only church in the area with a bell for announcing services, it also served government purposes by sounding air-raid alarms.

When the Woerners were assigned to teach at the Bible school in Wuchow (1936), Dr. Jaffray was the field director. This picture includes the faculty and students of the school; Gus and Pauline, front row. The man on the right end, front row is Walter Oldfield. (See Chapter 6.)

Gus was never one to sit at home, but was constantly itinerating in rural areas and always quick to lend a helping hand to anyone in need.

Raymond, 5, poses in front of the Bible school building in Wuchow with their family cook, Shih Er Ko, whom they affectionately called "Cook."

When Jaffray caught the vision to "go to the wild men of Borneo," the Woerners were invited to help him. Three years later, when an official invitation from the Indonesia conference arrived, they proceeded at once, leaving their children 2,000 miles away in MK school. Gus and Pauline arrived in Makassar on July 29, 1936. This picture was taken just before they left.

Dr. R.A. Jaffray, right, chairman of the South China, Indonesia and Malaya fields. Dr. R.A. Forrest, left, founder and first president of Toccoa Falls Institute, now Toccoa Falls College (TFC). In the Woerners' first year in Makassar, Forrest came to visit Indonesia. Gus had no idea at the time that within 8 years he would join Forrest at TFC.

L to R:
Gus Woerner,
Pauline Woerner,
Dr. R.A. Forrest,
in Makassar,
Indonesia (1936).

These former Borneo headhunters, having been transformed and now "beloved of God called to be saints," became church elders at Bethel Church (1938).

Because of increasingly unsettled conditions in the Far East, the Woerners made the difficult decision to leave their children in America when they returned to Indonesia in 1939. Gus' brother Fred, with 17 children of his own (9 still at home), offered to keep Robert, Ruth and Ray. Everyone, including the children, was at peace with the decision. It proved to be a wise one, for on December 7, 1941, Pearl Harbor was bombed and the Woerners were ordered to leave Malaya.

The faculty and students at the Makassar Bible School, Indonesia March 1937. *Kemah Indjil* means Gospel Tabernacle.

With the Makassar Bible School doing so well, Jaffray set his sights on building a second school at Ringlet in the Cameron Highlands of Malaya, about 400 miles north of Singapore. Gus became the administrator of the new station and principal of the school which was formerly a hotel. The primary purpose of the school was the reach the 40,000 Sakai people in the surrounding jungles.

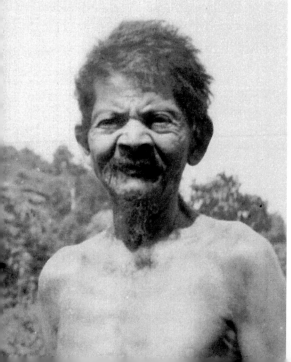

This man was one of the first Sakai converts. The Sakai were primitive people, fearing and running from outsiders. When they heard the gospel, they accepted eagerly. (Photograph supplied by the Alliance Archives; taken by Dr. Jaffray.)

金馬崙聖經學院師生合影<br>
辟

The faculty and students at the Ringlet Bible School, 1941, with Gus and Pauline seated center. In order to establish the school and accommodate the student body, dormitories were needed. With no earth-moving equipment nor money to hire workers, Gus began leveling the hilly ground by himself, using only a pick and shovel. Later, teachers and students helped to complete the project.

A church building had not yet been erected for this new Chinese congregation at Kuala Lipis, so they met in the pastor's home.

The Gustave Woerner family in 1976. Ray and his family on the left, Robert standing behind his parents, and Ruth (Good) and her family on the right. All three of the Woerner children became missionaries.

June 5, 1975 was a special occasion for Gus and Pauline as they celebrated 50 years of marriage at Toccoa Falls College.

Gus was asked to pray for this group of summer missionaries (1978), the first
to go from TFC. It was his last farewell. Moments later, at the back
of the auditorium, he collapsed and died.

Gus initiated a plan to provide housing for furloughing missionaries.
Ray Woerner and his family, on an extended leave from Chile, lived in
the first home Gus built on campus. It was washed away during the flood
of 1977. Ray's wife Betty Jean and his youngest daughter Debbie
perished. Since then, five more homes have been built. This one is
known as the Gus Woerner House.

In 1996, the million-dollar Woerner School of World Missions Center was dedicated on the Toccoa Falls College campus. The center was partially funded by Edward J. Woerner and Sons in honor of the Woerner family. Edward is the nephew of Gus and the son of Fred who took care of Gus' three children.

instant coffee, Dr. Jaffray asked, "Brother Woerner, do you know what came to me during the night?"

"What?"

"The devil tried to get me at Kalosi, but could not, so he is trying to get me now with this fever."

Still holding the kettle of water over the flame, Gus responded, "Dr. Jaffray, if you believe this fever is of the devil, God is going to heal you."

The thought struck Gus with such force that involuntarily he dropped the pot to the tile floor. Then he knelt to pray, calling on the Lord to rebuke Satan and heal Dr. Jaffray. From that moment, Jaffray began to improve, and within two days he was up and back to work.

But that was not the end of the story. During vacation time some of the Bible school students were usually sent to minister in Boegis territory. In past years, they had always come back discouraged. However, this year, since the encounter with the "prince of the Boegis tribe," the four students who were sent there later reported little opposition and even brought with them two young Boegis men to attend the Bible school!

One of the students was Ahmad Hind. Only seventeen, Ahmad was a bright and eager young man. However, within days his father and a chief from his town appeared at the school to take Ahmad home. Their excuse was that his mother was very ill with a fever and was calling for her son day and night.

The leaders at the school, thinking this was probably a hoax, asked Ahmad's father to sign a paper that he would allow his son to return. He would not. Ahmad did not want to go home, so his father took the matter to court.

"Do you want to go home with your father and the chief?" the judge asked Ahmad.

"No," he replied.

Noting the fervency of Ahmad's reply, the judge then asked, "Why do you want to study in this Bible school here in Makassar?"

"Because the Lord Jesus Christ called me to come and study to become a preacher of His gospel," came the firm reply.

"The only way you can take this boy out of school," the judge said, turning to Ahmad's father and the chief, "is if you appeal to your local rajah (king) and he brings the case to Makassar. The initial cost will be $25 and no telling how much more."

At this, the men turned on their heels and left. They never returned. Ahmad stayed in school and became one of the brightest and most diligent students Pauline Woerner ever had. A miracle had occurred! Satan, in the guise of one of his princes, had become an unwelcome visitor—and a defeated one!

The final group of visitors to Makassar was most welcome—the Woerner children. With 2,000 miles separating the family, it had been twelve months since they had seen each other. How much would the children have grown? How much would they have changed after another year of school? Gus and Pauline did not have long to wonder.

One of the teachers at the Wuchow Bible School wanted to visit Indonesia and stopped in Hong Kong to escort the Woerner children to Makassar. As the parents waited on the pier, they could see the children standing along the rail of the ship, waving white handkerchiefs. Soon they were in each others' arms. Pauline was ecstatic to have the children with her once again. Tears shone through her smiles.

"You haven't changed much," Gus exclaimed as he grinned and scanned their faces, "except Raymond—he's grown a lot."

Robert, Ruth and Raymond had been looking forward to coming to Makassar, their new home. Gus helped Ruth and Raymond learn to ride a bicycle. Since Robert had mastered that skill in Hong Kong, his goal was to ride up and down every street in Makassar. By the time he left for school in the fall, he had covered 117 streets and learned all their names!

It seemed inevitable that a whole summer could go by without at least one child having an accident. This time it was eight-year-old Ruth. While at the swimming pool one day she climbed to the top diving board to try to get a better view of a Java freighter that was pulling out of the harbor. Forgetting where she was, she stepped back and tumbled down the stairs to the cement below.

Gus and Pauline rushed to pick her up. At first it appeared that some serious damage had been done as her back was very painful. But X rays showed nothing broken. Still, she had to wear a cast for thirty-five long days—in the hot and humid tropics!

While the children were home, word came that things were not going well in China. Shanghai and other large cities in Central China were once again caught in the throes of war. Even Canton in South China was being bombed. However, as Hong Kong seemed to be safe and the Woerners had received no word to the contrary, on the first day of September the family was back on the wharf to say their good-byes. Of all the times they had been separated from their children, this one was the hardest, not only because of the troubles in China, but because the children wanted so much to stay with their parents.

"Why do we have to go back now?" Raymond asked. "Couldn't you just teach us at home?"

"Yes," Ruth coaxed. "We could help you sell books or mimeograph materials. Besides," she continued, "I still have to wear this old cast."

"Please let us stay just one semester," Robert chimed in. But sadly the parents had to say no. It was time for the children to go back to school in Hong Kong. And for Gus and Pauline, the fall

term of teaching in Makassar was about to begin.

As the boat pulled away from the dock, two
sad parents stood hand in hand watching and
waving until the tiny figures on the ship became
a distant blur. A lump rose in each throat—a
lump that could not be swallowed. Once again,
as in times past and times since, there was a
price to be paid for taking the gospel to the ends
of the earth.

## 12

# *To the Sakai*

It was January 1938 and time for the Woerners' second furlough. Seven years had passed since their parting from friends and family in the United States. They would have much to tell them about God's working in China and Indonesia.

Once all their affairs at the school were completed and arrangements were made for the opening of the new semester, the Woerners left for Makassar. From there, Pauline took a ship to Hong Kong to spend some extra time with the children before school closed and to have her tonsils removed and Ruth's as well on the same day.

While his wife and children were in Hong Kong, Gus headed for Malaya where missionaries Paul Fleming and Paul Lenn, together with Dr. Jaffray, were attempting to establish an evangelistic center among the primitive Sakai tribespeople. On his first trip to Indonesia, Dr. Jaffray had encountered small groups of this tribe. That time, they had run away in fright from the foreigner.

The Sakai dressed in meager jungle clothing complete with crude decorations. They sometimes wore torn trousers, but the most common attire was a dirty piece of cloth that was tied around their waists and reached to their feet. This tribe, about 40,000 strong, had never heard the name of Christ.

The Sakai (also called Senoi) had arrived on the Malay peninsula thousands of years B.C. Scattered over a large area and speaking several languages, the Sakai lived in longhouses, some of which were over ninety feet long and accommodated as many as sixty people. To escape marauding tigers and elephants, the houses were built on stilts thirty-nine inches to thirty feet high.

When the Malays came years later, they turned the Sakai into dependents and finally into slaves. In fact, the name Sakai literally means "infidel slave." It was the practice of the Indonesian slave owners to murder the adults and kidnap the children under nine years of age. Is it any wonder then that at the sight of strangers the Sakai would run away, climbing the nearest trees for safety?

As the missionaries pondered the challenge facing them, Gus thought, *Let's suppose the ninety and nine mentioned in the parable of the lost*

*sheep are those in so-called Christian lands who
have the gospel, and the lost sheep represent the heathen world. If the shepherd—Christ—would leave
the ninety-nine in the fold and go after the one lost
sheep until He found it, would He not want us today
to leave the comparatively few sheep at home and go
out to seek the millions in the world that are lost?
Shouldn't they too have the chance to hear and believe?*

To reach the Sakai, the first matter on the
agenda was to find a suitable place to locate a
settlement from which they could launch their
efforts. Paul Fleming had made an exploratory
trip to Kota Baru, a large city in the extreme
northeastern corner of British Malay, thinking it
might be a good base since other missionary
agencies had their headquarters to the south in
Singapore or Kuala Lumpur. However, at Kota
Baru there was no navigable river or highway,
not even a decent jungle trail to the interior. So
that was ruled out. However, some fifty miles
south of Kota Baru, on the east coast of the peninsula, was the town of Bertam, which was located at the mouth of the Nenggiri River. This
river, placid near the coast, was navigable for
about fifty miles upstream.

Paul Fleming secured an outboard motorboat
and, with Paul Lenn and two Makassar Bible
students, traveled the river until they found
what they thought would be a good place for a
station. At the site there were several Sakai
houses and ten to twenty more huts in a radius

of fifteen miles or so. These Sakai seemed friendly, and with their help the missionaries erected a small bamboo hut. They called it Tanjong Injil—Gospel Point. The missionaries left the two students there to hold services and begin visiting the outlying areas.

Now Gus had arrived. Since the two Pauls were planning a return trip to Gospel Point, they would take Gus with them. This time, though, the voyage would be very different.

As they entered the mouth of the Nenggiri River, it soon became obvious that this was not the "calm" season, as on the previous trip, but the "rough" or monsoon season. The first trip up the Nenggiri had taken half a day. There was no telling, with conditions as they were, how long this one would take.

Not thinking to take the season into account, the men loaded their baggage and supplies into a native boat in which they planned to complete their journey. The only man who knew the whims of the river was ill with a fever. So, counting on God's protection, the missionaries took their places in a boat manned by an unknown and unproven guide.

Slowly they rounded one bend after another, leaving familiar landmarks behind. The boat they were in required twenty inches of water in order to navigate safely. But the water level was lower than usual. Each time the boat scraped the bottom or hit a submerged rock, the propeller pin snapped. Fortunately, they had spare ones on board, but the delays were annoying. The first day's trip ended rather uneventfully except for the broken pins.

As darkness descended, the pilot pulled the vessel over to shore and secured it. The men gathered their supplies and hiked to a Malay hut where they cooked up a hearty meal of vegetables, rice, pork and tea before they retired for the night.

When the party awoke the next morning, they could not predict just how seriously the beauty of the day would be marred by its events. On the river once again, there were more delays because of broken propeller pins. The rapids were also more numerous and trying. It seemed that no sooner had one been navigated than another was waiting. Repeatedly, the motor failed and the boat slammed against the rocks, breaking the pin and thrusting the boat on a reckless ride down the rushing torrent. Poling and paddling desperately, the men were able each time to navigate the boat to shore where they could grab roots and branches and secure themselves long enough to insert the new pin. Sometimes the supplies had to be off-loaded to lighten the boat, then portaged over slippery rocks and jungle paths to the top of the rapids where they could once again be packed into the vessel.

During one of these encounters with the rapids, Paul Lenn fell into the white water. Instinctively, Paul Fleming jumped in to save both Lenn and the boat. Thankfully, he succeeded.

Some Malay fishermen, seeing their predicament, helped to pull the boat into shallow water for repairs.

By 6 p.m., all were exhausted. They stopped at another Malay shack for the night. The next morning, their host assured them that there was only one "serious" rapid between them and their destination. That rapid proved to be the longest, narrowest and crookedest rapid in the entire journey. At one point, the water flowed through an S-shaped channel with such force that it lifted the boat onto a submerged rock, leaving them virtually high but not very dry, the bow rising precipitously out of the water.

Terror stricken, the men waited for death—the ultimate finale to their battle with the river. But soon the force of the water released the boat and all hung on for dear life until they could bring it to shore. They had survived. It was a miracle!

At the end of their hair-raising journey there was still a twenty to twenty-five mile hike to Gospel Point. Bruised and bone-weary, they finally arrived safely at the Sakai station. What should have taken half a day had taken four days. It was one of the most hazardous trips Gus would ever experience.

Although the people in and around Gospel Point were generally unresponsive, the chief of the Sakai and eight men attended the nightly services. One evening after the meeting, Gus stepped outside the hut beyond the light of the Coleman lamp. Looking up at the night sky, he thought, *The devil has succeeded in keeping the gospel from these Sakai for centuries, and he surely tried to keep us from getting up the river. But praise to our glorious Lord, Satan could not defeat or destroy us on our journey. God is reaching out to the Sakai too.*

After several days at Gospel Point, the group decided not to entrust their lives again to the treacherous waters of the river. Instead, they would walk out to the closest railroad station. The two young Bible students were left behind to explore the outlying settlements of the Sakai and to hold services. The missionaries assured the students that they would not forget them, but that they would be searching for a better location for a station, perhaps near the railroad where travel would not be limited by the vagaries of the seasons.

At dawn the men began their trek. Starting early would allow them to get some distance behind them before it got too hot. It would also mean that they would get to the train station before dark. The jungle path, barely discernible in the dense underbrush, could hardly be called a path. In Borneo, such paths were referred to as "rat trails."

The roots, stones and mud made walking difficult. By 10 a.m. Paul Fleming had developed such blisters on his feet that Paul Lenn had to serve as his crutch for the rest of the journey. Since Lenn was also carrying a twelve-gauge Winchester repeating shotgun and a twenty-gauge, single-barrel shotgun, both in canvas bags, Gus offered to relieve him of the burden. Tying the gun cases together, he slung them over his shoulder with the barrels pointing backward. He started off down the trail at his normal gait.

About noon, he noticed a log beside the path. *This would be a good place to rest and wait for the others*, he thought to himself. Just before sitting down, he let the front (butt) ends of the guns drop to the ground. Somehow the hammer of the shotgun cocked itself as he let the guns down. As it hit the ground, the gun fired. A bullet tore through the leather cap of the case, hit the edge of Gus' pith helmet and whizzed by his head about two inches from his left ear.

Flashes of Dr. Jaffray's encounter with the "prince of the Boegis tribe" blazed through his mind. Could this nearly fatal "accident" have been the work of the "prince of the Sakai tribe"? It was evident from the trip up the river that "someone" was trying to destroy the men and frustrate their efforts. Was this gun incident just another attack? Gus bowed his head and prayed that the power of Satan would be broken, that the Holy Spirit would break through and that the Sakai would be evangelized.

His prayer was answered. Sometime later, a Sakai chief attended services conducted by Paul Lenn and Paul Fleming. This was significant, for if the chief became a believer and was baptized, many of his people would follow his lead. The powers of darkness were defeated and many of the Sakai did become children of God.

What a joy and relief it was for Gus to arrive safely back in Singapore and reunite with Pauline and the children. After taking some time off for a little sightseeing, they boarded the *SS Bremen* and sailed for the United States.

Furlough year passed quickly and, as their return to Indonesia approached, the most troubling question now facing Gus and Pauline was "What should we do with the children during this next term?" Difficult as the decision was, both of them felt that the children should be left in the United States because of the unsettled conditions in the Far East. The Sino-Japanese conflict was still raging. Threats of war were on every side. Dr. Jaffray kept himself well informed on political developments around the world and talked freely about the possibility of another world war. He was sure that Japan would be one of the antagonists. The troubling part about that was the proximity of Japan to both Indonesia and Hong Kong. Yes, the Woerners decided, the children must be left in the United States in order to insure their safety. But with whom?

A couple in Detroit volunteered to take them into their home if no other solution could be found. Then Gus' sister Gertrude, who had two children of her own, offered to keep them. Finally, Gus' brother Fred, not knowing of the other offers, asked if he and his wife could help. Fred and Emma lived on the old Woerner homestead where Gus had grown up. They had seventeen children of their own; the younger nine were still at home. Fred's wife Emma was even more excited about the prospect of adding to her brood than Fred himself. One day she laughingly told Gus and Pauline, "I've always wanted to work in an orphanage!" Now she would have one of her own! To their own nine children still at home, they gladly added Robert, thirteen, Ruth, ten and Raymond, eight.

Everyone felt that on the farm in Elberta, Alabama, with Uncle Fred and Aunt Emma, was the place the Lord wanted the children. And everyone, including the children themselves, seemed at peace with the decision.

To accommodate so many children, a dozen beds were placed head to foot, lining the sleeping porch that wrapped around the front and side of the house. Here the boys slept in all but the coldest weather. The girls slept in one room in the house.

Twice a day Grandma Woerner prayed. The first was at meal times when there was always a German blessing before eating, and afterward Fred read a Bible passage and explained it. The table, always generously laden with nourishing food and surrounded by fifteen or twenty people, seemed like a perpetual banquet.

The second time Grandma Woerner prayed was at bedtime when everyone met together for devotions. Ruth played the piano and everyone sang from the hymnbook. Then, about half of the Bible was read (or so it seemed to the children), followed by prayer with many participating. When it was time for Grandma to pray, everyone got comfortable—Grandma's German conversations with the Lord were very long! These prayers, however, had a great influence on the lives of all her children and grandchildren.

When the time came to return to Indonesia, Gus and Pauline attended a service at the Gospel Tabernacle in New York City where they were members. Gus' brother Carl, who was also there, requested that the congregation sing the hymn "Majestic Sweetness Sits Enthroned."

> To Him I owe my life and breath,
> And all the joys I have;
> He makes me triumph over death,
> And saves me from the grave.

"And saves me from the grave." Those words somehow seemed to etch themselves in Gus' mind. He could not erase them from his thoughts the rest of the day. What did it mean? What could they mean? Perhaps that they were to embark on a term of service potentially more hazardous than the former two? Perhaps danger lurked ahead, but they would be kept by God's supernatural power? Gus wasn't sure.

That night as they went to bed, Pauline said to Gus, "Do you know what impressed me most while singing that hymn that Carl requested this morning? It was the words, 'And saves me from the grave.' " Just days later they would understand more fully the significance of that phrase.

While traveling through Kentucky on their way to Elberta a few days later, the car skidded on a slippery road. Gus tried to gain control of the vehicle as it whipped around on the pavement. Finally, after spinning two complete revolutions, it came to a stop on the brink of a steep mountain precipice. Had it gone over into the gorge, all five Woerners would have been killed. Why or how it had stopped at that point no one ever knew. What they did know was that in a miraculous way God had truly saved them all "from the grave." Once the car settled, Gus looked up. Amazingly, the vehicle was headed in their original direction.

Another service back in New York some weeks later proved to be a blessing as well. Dr. Lee Olsen, the choir director, had a wonderful surprise for the Woerners. Remembering that Gus had talked about the pastor of a church in Makassar who had been a bandmaster before he became a Christian, Olsen presented the Woerners with ten band instruments, including a bass drum. He even added a gift of money to cover the shipping charges.

Gus was overjoyed. He could already envision the excitement when he would present the instruments to the pastor. These beautiful instruments would make glorious music compared to the bamboo ones, the only ones the congregation was able to afford.

Now it was time to leave. Gus' prayer for his children was that they would learn some of the lessons he had learned on that old farm and in that same old house. Although he knew that Fred and Emma could not take the place of father and mother to his children, he and Pauline had the utmost confidence in them.

A wonderful and unexpected gift to take to the field with them was the gift of a car, a six-cylinder Ford, given to them by Gus' brother Carl, the same brother who had sacrificed his share of the bicycle money for the rebuilding of the Toccoa Falls Institute more than twenty-six years earlier. Since he could not go overseas himself, he said, the car would represent him on the field.

As he presented the car to Gus, Carl said, "First, I sent half a bicycle to Toccoa Falls; now I'm sending a car to the mission field."

"Don't forget—you are also sending your brother," Gus reminded him.

"Oh, that's right—and my brother," Carl added with a smile.

Fred had also been supportive of Gus in many ways—lending him vehicles to use on furlough, and, when the Woerners came home to stay, giving him a piece of land and a house. Fred had wanted to be a missionary, but stayed home to care for their mother. One thing he could do was to help Gus, Pauline and their family.

The decision to leave the children in Alabama proved to be a wise one. For on December 7, 1941, Pearl Harbor was bombed and the Woerners were ordered to leave Malaya. They could only imagine what would have happened to the children if they had been in Hong Kong.

# 13

# *A Bible School for Ringlet*

After weeks of strenuous deputation, the ocean voyage, this time wonderfully free of seasickness, was a welcome and delightful time of relaxation for Gus and Pauline despite the ache of separation from the children that lingered in their hearts.

Gus, however, was not idle. On board, he held a series of Bible classes, then in Honolulu conducted a midweek service and in Manila lectured to the Bible school students. Ministry was his passion, the thing that brought most pleasure to his heart.

Several days after the Woerners arrived in Hong Kong, conditions became so tense that the various consuls urged their women and children to evacuate. That meant that the Alliance hostel might be closed. Once again, Gus and Pauline were relieved that their children were safe and sound in the United States.

While home on furlough, they had been appointed to Singapore by the Indonesian Conference to assist in the launching of a Bible school. Upon arriving in Hong Kong, however, they received a cablegram from Dr. Jaffray requesting them to come to Makassar first. The Woerners thought this a bit strange, but when they arrived at Makassar and greeted Dr. Jaffray, they realized he not only wanted to go over his plans for the Bible school but really just wanted some fellowship with his "right-hand man." Gus would be in charge of building and administering the school.

Jaffray had chosen Makassar (now Ujung Pandang) as his base of operations because it was central to reaching the entire Indonesian archipelago. Now, with the Makassar Bible School and church doing well and growing, it was time to move on.

"We need another school, this time in Malaya," Jaffray told Gus, "and you are the man to head this work."

*It's a good thing we're not assigned to Makassar just now*, Gus thought to himself. He had heard over the ship's radio en route from Hong Kong to Makassar that England and France had declared war on Germany. *Singapore is British and, since I was born in Germany, it's probably better not to be going there.*

While in Makassar Gus and Pauline also personally delivered the musical instruments Lee Olsen had sent for the Makassar Gospel Tabernacle. Thankfully, the customs official had not opened the cases nor demanded taxes. The Lord had taken care of it all.

To minister in Malaya, the Woerners needed visas. Although acquiring visas was not a problem, there was another major hurdle. Just two days earlier, an order had been given that no more visas would be issued for Singapore. Faced with a dilemma that had no apparent human solution, Gus and Pauline presented the situation to the Lord and waited for His answer.

A few days later, after consultation between Dr. Jaffray and the highest government officials, the Woerners were issued visas and proceeded to Singapore, praising God for His intervention.

It was decided that the new Bible school would be situated in Ringlet, Cameron Highlands, about 400 miles north of Singapore, beyond Gospel Point and Kuala Lumpur. Gus would be the administrator of the new station.

His first order of business was to finalize transfer of a property which Dr. Jaffray had chosen earlier. Mr. Stacy, the owner of the property known as the Brooklands Private Hotel, was eager to dispose of it. His asking price was $25,000. Jaffray told Gus he could probably buy it for $20,000 and gave him authority to do so.

The negotiations in Gus's own words were as follows:

Sensing the owner wanted to dispose of the property quickly so he could retire to England, I started by offering $18,000. To my surprise, he agreed to the figure. Then an unknown difficulty arose. According to the law of the Malay government, no organization or firm could purchase real estate in its name. So I could not buy the property in the name of The Christian and Missionary Alliance.

Then I tried to buy it in Dr. Jaffray's name, but their law stated no one could buy it in another person's name. Finally, I purchased it in my own name. Immediately I notified Dr. Jaffray and asked what to do next. He told me to let it stand for the time being and get on with the plans for the work of the Alliance in Malaya.

These plans were threefold. The primary goal was to reach the 40,000 Sakai scattered throughout the mountainous jungles in the interior of the Malay Peninsula. Four stations had already been established—Jalong, Ringlet, Temengor and Betis. All of them were isolated since the Sakai did not inhabit populated areas nor mingle with other races.

The second objective was to endeavor to visit systematically the many large towns in the lowlands of the peninsula with a gospel tent which had been secured while the Woerners were on furlough. Paul Fleming and two Chinese pastors from the Chinese Foreign Missionary Society were already overseeing nightly meetings in the region where there were over 2 million Chinese, many of them unevangelized.

The third goal was to start a Bible school at Ringlet to train the newly converted Sakai and Chinese who felt called into ministry. The opening of the school seemed to be a priority because of the great revival taking place among them. It was a formidable task, considering that Dr. Jaffray's initial visit to the area had taken place just two years before.

Since the buildings of the Brooklands Private Hotel were standing empty, the Woerners were permitted to occupy them even before the transaction was complete. There were still three servants living there and for several weeks Gus and Pauline felt like millionaires.

When the district government official heard that a Bible school was about to open, he came to look over the situation. He finally informed Gus that government permission was required in order to operate an educational institution.

"Furthermore," he stated, "I don't see a school building. You'll have to provide something more satisfactory along that line too."

Gus had hoped they could improvise with what they had.

"What you have will not pass government inspection," the officer added brusquely.

Gus and the others working with him were disappointed, but Gus assured them that this was only a delay, not a denial. They would pray for wisdom about how to open the school and that the Lord would give them favor with the government to expedite the process.

After the officer's visit, Gus became even more certain that God wanted him to open a school where God's Word could be taught. A suitable but very hilly location for two dormitories was found. The land had to be cleared and graded before construction could begin. But how does one remove so many cubic yards of dirt from a hill that slopes about four feet in every ten?

"Lord, what shall we do?" Gus pleaded. "There are no funds to hire workers to move all this dirt."

"You start," God answered. And so he did. Singlehandedly, with a pick and shovel, Gus began the tedious task.

About that time, six young Chinese men appeared, thinking they could begin studies at the school. They were so amazed to see Gus, a teacher, doing manual labor that they asked to help. Gus offered them coolie wages and they dug in, literally. In the midst of it all, three weeks of Bible classes were held for the workers. Their spare time, even for the two Chinese teachers, was spent leveling the terrain. Gus praised God for their dedication to the Savior and His cause.

Between teaching and digging, the Woerners visited the areas around Ringlet and ministered to the Sakai. One trip would have been only seventy miles over jungle paths, but more than 200 miles by road. Gus and Pauline chose the road, and thanked God every mile for Carl and their new car.

But Pauline was not satisfied. For a long time she had wanted to visit the Sakai hidden in the depths of the jungle. She enjoyed shorter trips by car, but she felt left out, not having seen how this tribe actually lived so far away from civilization. The next time Gus was planning to go to the Sakai via the jungle, Pauline asked to accompany him.

"But, Pauline," Gus stuttered, "you don't know how hard such a trip will be. You've heard me tell of the dangers and hardships . . ."

Pauline interrupted.

"I'm going," she said with finality. "I'll wear good shoes. I can take it."

So, early one morning some weeks later, Gus and Pauline started on their jungle journey. The first 250 miles were by car. That night they stopped at a Chinese hotel. Pauline was glad for the delicious meal and good sleep. The next morning they secured the services of a Sakai carrier and headed off on foot. The first three miles were easy as they walked through a rubber estate. Then they came to a small river which could be crossed only by squatting in a small dugout.

Safely on the other side, the Woerners faced a path that was vastly different from what Pauline had experienced so far on the journey. She had to scramble over huge jungle trees and walk on logs much like a tightrope walker in a circus. For several miles the sun beat down on them unmercifully as they plunged through felled trees and tangled brush. What a relief it was finally to enter virgin jungle again and arrive at a tribal hut surrounded by several coconut trees. A worker volunteered to scale one of the trees and throw down fresh coconuts to the travelers. How delicious and refreshing the milk tasted! After paying the Sakai five cents apiece for the coconuts, the party continued on.

Mile after mile they trudged over a rough and narrow path, stumbling over roots and hearing the cries of wild animals in the distance. Some hours later, they reached the hut where they were to spend the night. After climbing a crude ladder into the thatch-roofed structure, they fell wearily into bed, even though the bed was the floor. Nevertheless, they slept well.

The next morning Pauline awoke, surprised at her surroundings. Her eyes scanned the crude and simple walls. No nails had been used in its construction. Jungle trees had been used for poles and tree bark for the walls and floor. The roof was made of palm leaves. The kitchen, such as it was, was a sixteen-square-foot space in one corner of the single room. Its floor was covered with clay and in the center several large stones held a big black cooking pot. There were no chairs, tables or beds—the floor served for all.

Gus and Pauline shared the gospel with the tribespeople and taught them some choruses. In this, her first long trip into the jungles, Pauline felt God's reassurance that they would see Him work mightily among the Sakai. They were not to be disappointed.

Back at Ringlet, the workers finished the project of leveling the dormitory sites and, by the end of December, they had also received government permission not only to open the school, but also to obtain a temporary license for two acres of land in the Bera Lake area where they would build a bamboo house for the district workers. Now they too had a place to live and a new area was opened for the gospel.

God was once again doing more than the Woerners could ask or even think. But what did the future hold?

The Cameron Highlands Bible School opened early in 1941. True, the rumblings of war and the power of Japan's military forces were unsettling but seemed far off. Surely at the Bible school all were safe.

Or were they?

# 14

# *Plan B*

Gus believed that the best, the only, way to evangelize a neglected area was through national workers. While missionaries are often necessary to open new works and train nationals, local churches cannot come into being, develop or prosper without the ministry of national personnel. The ministry of the new Bible school at Ringlet was critical to train those nationals to become leaders and pastors in the local churches.

Even before permission was granted to open the school, Rev. Simon Meek, a Chinese pastor in the Philippines, heard about the Ringlet station.

"I'd like to hold a Keswick-style deeper life conference at Ringlet," he told Gus. "There will be about twenty-five to thirty in attendance."

Gus agreed that the group could come, provided each person would bring his or her own gear. He also approached the markets in Ringlet about their need for rice and other staples to feed thirty people. Imagine Gus' surprise when more than sixty Chinese arrived. Although there had to be some last-minute rearranging and soliciting for food, the conference was a huge success. Gus viewed it as a sign for good.

February 19, 1941, was a red-letter day at Ringlet. It was on that day that Gus officiated at the opening of the Cameron Highlands Bible School of The Christian and Missionary Alliance—one year after the date originally intended. The school boasted four teachers: Gus and Pauline and two Chinese teachers.

Unexpected and interesting experiences became the norm at Ringlet. The Woerners never knew what a day might bring.

One day a man who had been addicted to drugs for thirty-seven years arrived on the compound hoping to kick the habit. Gus and some students took turns staying with the man, spending hours in prayer for him as the craving made the poor wretch scream, writhe, toss himself on the floor or bed and beat himself. One night a wild bird flew into the room, then out again. For some reason the addict felt that this was God's way of telling him he was delivered. And he was.

Another time, Gus was resting one Sunday afternoon when there was a loud knock on his door. He opened it to find a student wanting to be baptized "right now." He was afraid to wait, he said, for fear he might die and be lost. Gus paused.

"Baptism in itself will not save you," he explained. But the man assured Gus that he really was born again. He simply wanted to be obedient to God's Word. Gus then took him and some of his friends down to a hole among the boulders in a nearby creek and baptized him in what came to be known as the "boulder baptistry."

On a mid-August afternoon, Gus went into town on business. When he picked up his mail at the post office, one envelope drew his immediate attention. It contained the sad news that his sister-in-law Emma had passed away suddenly after a severe heart attack.

While this in itself was sad news, Gus and Pauline were concerned because this was the woman whom their children were now calling Mama. However, Fred, Gus's brother and Emma's husband, assured them that he had no thought of asking them to make other arrangements or to turn the children over to anyone else.

A side effect of Emma's death reached all the way to the students at the Bible school. An informal "get-together merry meeting" planned for that evening turned instead into a memorial and prayer service characterized by a real spirit of revival.

On November 14, 1941, the first full year of operation for the Cameron Highlands Bible School came to a close with blessings too many to count.

Though Holland had been conquered by Germany in 1940, giving some reason for serious apprehension, the war raging in Europe did not seem to reach the Far East until December 16, 1941. That day dawned with a few pink and golden clouds on the horizon, the promise of a beautiful day. But it became a day never to be forgotten by the Woerners. Because the Japanese were continuing their relentless drive down the Malay Peninsula, the Woerners and hundreds of others living in the Cameron Highlands were ordered to evacuate to Singapore.

About to be torn from the station and the work that was so dear to their hearts, Gus and Pauline frantically searched for a local radio station with news from home. The news was grim. Pearl Harbor had been attacked and America's fleet of warships severely damaged. A special announcement said that on the northern frontiers of Malaya, British troops were fighting valiantly against the Germans. In fact, the British had been cut off by the infiltration tactics of the Japanese. One part of a coded message read: "You are not forgotten."

Although meant for the troops, this little sentence was of great comfort to Gus and Pauline as well. The Japanese had landed only about 100 miles from Ringlet. Thailand had already capitulated. The ill-fated *HMS Prince of Wales* and *Repulse* had been sunk, Penang had fallen and, on the sixth day of the war, had been evacuated in wild confusion. The Japanese, they heard, were already beginning to bomb and to perform stunts over the airdome in Ipoh, only thirty miles from Ringlet.

In the words of Gus:

> Everything around us seemed to be going under. No word from our headquarters in New York City nor from our beloved chairman Dr. Jaffray in Makassar. Nor was any mail coming through from our dear children and friends in the States. And there we were alone, the only two Alliance missionaries in the jungles of Malaya and the Japanese coming closer every hour. Do you wonder if we began to think we were forgotten? But God is never too late. "You are not forgotten," said the code to the soldiers, and God told us that neither were we.

A sergeant of the local defense corps pulled up at their little post in a Fiat, a Colt automatic resting on his hip. In no uncertain tones he announced: "All European [white] women and children must be off the Highlands by 2 p.m.

and in Kuala Lumpur [150 miles away] before dark tonight."

Before anyone could move, the official turned to Gus and continued: "I'll let you know directly whom you're to take in your car. Each one," he added, "may take one, or at the most two small suitcases." With that he left.

Practically everything the Woerners owned, together with the equipment of the Missionary Rest Home and the Bible school, had to be left behind. Going into the village store, Gus called the district officer to see if he could make an exception in their case. Since they were missionaries, Gus told him they had no desire to leave their station and were prepared to stay on at their own risk, even it it meant falling into enemy hands and being cut off from the rest of the allied world for "the duration."

The only response Gus got was that the officer had no authority to countermand military orders. With that, he hung up.

Three extra adults, two small children and their bundles were assigned to the Woerner car. With everybody and everything finally loaded, they started down the serpentine mountain road. Since they had been warned that they could be forced off the road at anytime, they took a blanket, mosquito net and some food and drinking water. Fortunately, the car had just been serviced and the tank was full of gas. After a long and nerve-racking trip, they arrived safely in Kuala Lumpur just as the blackout lamps were being lighted in the city.

The next eight days were spent there. If they "stayed put" and if conditions improved, they were told, they might return to Ringlet in a few days. However, conditions only worsened. At great risk, Martahan, one of the Mission's faithful workers from Ringlet, was able to get through to Kuala Lumpur and brought Gus the Mission books, important papers, pictures of the work and some Bible study notes. He arrived just before Ringlet was cut off from the outside world.

As Martahan handed Gus' teaching and preaching notes to him, he said, "Teacher, the war is too bad and you won't get to return. You will want these." Gus could barely express his appreciation, so moved was he by the selflessness and daring of the young man.

"I almost wished that I could shed my white skin for a black one," Gus said, "for then I could have returned with him and stayed on. Being white, however, this was impossible—a strange and stern reality."

Several days later the Woerners were told to go to Singapore. Although many cars were seized by the military, the Woerners still had theirs and were able to drive. They finally sold the car for almost as much as it had cost three years earlier.

It was Christmas Eve when they arrived in
Singapore. Christmas Day was the same as any
other except that leaflets were dropped on the
city wishing the white man a Merry Christmas—but no Happy New Year!

At the consular office, the Woerners were informed that a ship was leaving in a few days.
There were a limited number of berths still available. In fact, the consul had tentatively placed
their names on the booking list since they were
now considered refugees. Fortunately the bank
was able to transfer their personal accounts to
Singapore. They did not lose the Mission funds
nor their personal money. With this money and
the receipts from the sale of the car, they were
able to buy tickets to Panama and then home to
Alabama. Though they had lost all, God supplied their need just at the right time.

Years earlier, when Gus and Pauline had been
accepted as missionaries with the Alliance, they
understood that it would be for life. They had no
thought of ever coming home other than on regular furlough. They expected to die or be caught
up to heaven from the mission field.

Now, though forced to leave their station, the
Woerners were nevertheless troubled in their
hearts, fearing that if they went home, they
would be stepping out of the will of God. There
was nothing they feared more than that.

However, when Gus heard via coded message
that Plan B was in effect for the soldiers, he was
comforted. "God's will is in sections," he wrote,

"and one section is as much His will as the other. Plan A of the will of God was that we get to the mission field, and our enforced leaving was His Plan B. So we will accept our lot from God with gratitude. In our case, the Lord is simply shifting us from one sector of the fighting front to another, from Malaya to the United States. We are still in the will of God. Praise His name."

# 15

# Doors Opened— Doors Closed

**P**auline and Gus stood on the deck of the ship gazing sadly at the sliver of land disappearing in the distance.

"It's so hard to leave, isn't it?" Pauline sighed, wiping away a tear. "We were just really getting the school at Ringlet under way."

"Yes, my dear," her husband responded. "We had such high hopes." Gus took a deep, unsteady breath.

"Just think, Pauline," he assured her, "we're safely away from the Japanese army for now. Think how good the Lord has been to us! In and out we have moved, through doors the Lord has opened and closed just at the right time, without a hitch and without a scratch. We've lost everything except that small suitcase, but all our needs have

been supplied. We've been unable to plan anything, but everything has been worked out for us."

"Strange," she murmured, as her eyes focused
on a misty spot above the far horizon.

"No, not strange—wonderful!"

The voyage home to the States was unlike any
other they had ever taken. It was wartime, and
there were blackouts from dusk to dawn. Life-
boats were provisioned and ready in case of an
emergency. Passengers carried their life jackets
with them at all times. Air raid and emergency
drills were staged regularly. Tension filled the
decks and staterooms.

On February 15, 1942, after forty-eight long
days aboard ship, the Woerners finally arrived in
Panama. Just two days earlier, Makassar, the Alliance headquarters in Indonesia, had gone up
in flames. Six missionaries and Dr. Jaffray had
fallen prisoner to the Japanese. Singapore too
had fallen. (See *The Pearl and the Dragon*, Book
17 in The Jaffray Collection of Missionary Portraits.)

As their ship pulled into the New Orleans harbor, Gus and Pauline strained to see the familiar
faces of their children and other family members. Finally focused, their broad smiles brought
tears to Gus and Pauline's eyes. What a welcome sight! It did not matter that all were being
drenched by a driving rain.

To welcome them home, Fred, along with
Gus and Pauline's children and several of his
own, had driven the 200 miles from Elberta

through pouring rain in a covered truck, everyone huddled under blankets, miserable and
cold. At first the children were refused admis-
sion to the shipyard and were forced to stand in
the pounding rain until a watchman noticed
their feet as he looked out under the warehouse
door. Taking pity on them, he raised the door
enough for them to get inside and enjoy a ring-
side view of the ship's arrival.

"How you have all grown!" Pauline exclaimed
after there were hugs all around. "I can hardly
recognize you, Robert. You're taller than I am."

Bob smiled shyly.

"It's been a long time, Mother. I grew up
while we were apart!"

It did not take the Woerners long to realize
that their children had grown spiritually as well.
Gus' heart was filled with a big debt of gratitude
to Fred and Emma. They had provided a good
and godly home for the children. They had done
well.

"Please bless and reward him, Lord, for the
kindness and love he and his wife showed us and
our children," Gus whispered to the Lord.

Although Gus and Pauline were now safe at
home and profoundly thankful to God to be
there, in spirit they were still in Ringlet. The first
school year had ended with fourteen students.
Had the war not interfered, there would have
been at least thirty the following term. They
could not forget the work and their fellow work-

ers with whom they longed to be. They had given all the money they could spare to the ones that were left at Ringlet. It would be sufficient to provide their allowances through the following February.

After the Woerners arrived in Elberta, they received several letters from Malaya, written before Singapore fell. The preaching of the gospel was continuing even though the missionaries had had to leave.

"Perhaps," Pauline commented, "the national workers will now develop the sense of responsibility and leadership which we were hoping to see them attain."

"Yes," Gus agreed, "and if, in the providence of God, the war ends favorably, you and I are ready to go back at anytime."

"Nothing would give me greater joy," Pauline responded.

Gus agreed, adding, "But whether in Ringlet or here, let us serve the Lord well!"

Meanwhile, Fred invited Gus and Pauline to live on the home place for the time being. Gus felt as though he was coming back to his Bethel, his boyhood home. It also provided a comfortable setting for the family to spend their first few months together.

A few weeks later, while they were attending a retreat near Toccoa, Georgia, Dr. Forrest asked Gus and Pauline if they would consider coming to Toccoa Falls Institute (TFI) to serve on the faculty as head of the missions department for the duration of the war or furlough, whichever came first.

Gus told Dr. Forrest that their time belonged primarily to the Alliance. Forrest understood, but pointed out that the school did not operate on a semester basis, but on five seven-week periods. He would be able to use the Woerners one or two of those periods when they were not itinerating. In the light of that, and since Dr. Forrest was a member of the Alliance Board of Managers, Gus told him that any arrangement he could make with the board would be satisfactory to him.

Another concern facing the Woerners was the education of their children. Dr. Forrest suggested that, since Gus and Pauline had consented to teach at the college, the Institute would take care of Robert's education. Mother Woerner was very happy to see them going to the school she called "God's Bible School," the school for which she had prayed so earnestly after the disastrous fire of 1913.

So, in the summer of 1944, the family moved to Toccoa Falls. Since there was no campus housing for them, Gus and Pauline occupied a small apartment on the second floor of Gate Cottage at the base of beautiful Toccoa Falls. The children lived in various dormitories. The family ate their meals together in the Institute dining room.

In the fall the Woerners received two letters from Malaya. One man told about the work he was doing with the Sakai and that he was praying the war would soon end so that Gus and Pauline could return. Another, from Paul Lenn, also brought good news—he was still teaching in the Bible school in Ringlet.

The following summer while Gus was ministering at the Old Orchard campground in Maine, he heard that World War II had ended. He also received the sad news that Dr. Jaffray had passed away in a Japanese prison camp, exchanging the cross he had borne for nearly half a century for his crown. The date was July 29, 1945.

Of Dr. Jaffray, Gus wrote:

> Words fail me to express adequately my deep appreciation of the man of God and leader of missionaries. Of all the ministerial brethren and fellow missionaries I have known, he has influenced my life more than any other individual. It was my privilege to serve the Lord on the mission fields of South China, Indonesia and Malaya under this outstanding missionary statesman, pioneer and spiritual leader.

Gus suffered another loss the following year. Before he left for the spring convention tour, his eighty-one-year-old mother had begun to show signs of weakening physically though not spiritually. As she bade her son farewell, she said, "Gustave, if the Lord calls me home before your tour is finished, do not leave it and come home to walk behind my coffin."

Mother Woerner must have had some kind of premonition that the time of her departure was near. Halfway through his tour, Gus received a call from Dr. Forrest stating that she had passed away.

"What are you going to do?" Forrest asked him.

When told that Gus would not leave the tour because of his mother's wishes, Dr. Forrest said, "Then may I take your three children, two nieces and one nephew (all students at TFI) to Elberta to attend the funeral?"

"If you are free and could do it, I would be very glad," Gus answered. It was done.

After living on the second floor of Gate Cottage for a year, the Woerners made the second of several moves to different living quarters. This time, with their apartment needed for dormitory space, they moved to a small apartment at the rear of Ralls Dormitory, which housed male students. They felt it was the least they could do in order to make room for more students to train as missionaries.

Later that year the Woerners received a letter from Alliance headquarters in New York City saying that the Mission had decided to withdraw from Malaya. Gus and Pauline were disappointed, but accepted the news as God's will.

Pauline and Gus responded:

Thus far we have been holding ourselves in readiness to return to Malaya as soon as conditions permitted. We were naturally disappointed, but accepted it as from the Lord, all being included in Plan B and whatever that involved. At first it meant leaving Malaya. Now it evidently means staying where the Lord has brought us. "Praise His Name anyhow," a motto on my desk says. Besides, with the needs of TFI and the opportunities here, we feel at this time we ought to remain where we are and do what we can for the Mission and the school.

Plan B was in effect.

# 16

# *Missions—*
# *a Family Affair*

Gustave and Pauline Woerner may have been living in North America, but their passion for reaching the lost had not diminished. Called a "missionary for all seasons" and dedicated to the Lord from birth, Gus' life could be divided into three parts: preparing for the mission field, serving on the mission field and preparing students at Toccoa Falls Institute (now Toccoa Falls College) to answer the call to the mission field.

On January 1, 1949, the names of Gustave and Pauline Woerner were removed from the list of missionaries on allowance. Although this event brought Plan A to an official conclusion, the Woerners' reaction reflected their acceptance of the board's decision.

"We thank the Lord," they wrote, "that the change of status means only the end of a chapter, not the end of the book. Our hearts are still burdened for the Sakai tribespeople in Malaya. If the door is closed to that field and we must join the ranks of the workers at home, we earnestly desire and pray to be just as enthusiastic and faithful in serving the Lord in Plan B as we were in Plan A.

"There is a definite need here with wonderful opportunities in the missions department of the Bible college, for which our missionary service and experience of nearly twenty years have aptly fitted us. We consider it a great honor and joy to have the privilege of assisting at TFI in the training of young people for Christian service. . . ."

Now that the Woerners could give their full time to TFI, one of the first things Dr. Forrest did was to make Gus a member of the executive committee of the Institute. Gus also sponsored the Foreign Missions Fellowship, a student organization that met weekly. And he was chairman of the spiritual life committee which arranged for chapel speakers and had oversight of the Sunday services. In addition, he carried a load of fifteen to twenty hours of classroom work per week.

At this time Gus acquired a new title. It came about because of the three daughters and two sons of Fred who had, over a number of years, been students at TFI. Naturally they called their uncle "Uncle Gus." The other students picked up the name, and even when Fred's children graduated, most of the students and many of the faculty continued to use that term of endearment. Since "Uncle" is a rather affectionate title, Gus felt greatly honored.

When Gus began to teach at TFI, only one missions course was offered. He soon added a second, then a third which eventually resulted in an entire missions studies curriculum. Gus' ability to instill in the hearts of his students the zeal to reach the lost in far-off lands was unique. That ability was based on the belief that because of the overwhelming need overseas, all who were able should consider that ministry a first priority.

"Don't wait for a call to go to the regions beyond," he often told his students. "You are called to go unless you are called to stay home. Read the great commission in the Bible. It doesn't say to wait for a call—it says 'Go!' "

It soon became obvious that Gus was having a profound impact on the school and its constituency. Students enrolled in missions courses found themselves in classes unlike any others on their schedules. As they walked into the classroom, they sensed an atmosphere of enthusiasm and anticipation because Gus was not just teaching—he was encouraging his students to accept their responsibility to take the message of salvation to the four corners of the world.

Whether he was using examples from his own experiences or biblical principles or illustrations,

Gus always quoted from Scripture to summarize the idea he was trying to impress on his hearers. One example came from a memorable incident in Indonesia. While visiting in West Borneo, he had gone with the local missionary to inspect some materials that had been gathered to build an 800-seat church. The men soon noticed black clouds rising above the jungle ceiling, so they started back to the chapel. On the way they passed some Dyaks returning to their homes. One family, with the father holding a baby, approached the missionaries and stopped directly in front of them on the path.

"Our baby is very sick. Will you pray that the Lord will heal her?" he asked the men.

Remembering the dark cloud, Gus said, "Let's go back to the chapel or we will get drenched and maybe the baby will get pneumonia and die. We will pray there."

Hearing this, the father asked, "How long does it take God to answer prayer?"

How ashamed and rebuked Gus felt—he, the missionary, talking as though God was unable spontaneously to answer prayer. Immediately he prayed both for himself and for the child. And they all went on their way rejoicing.

The next Sunday, the family was in church. The baby was perfectly well!

Another illustration Gus used was so powerful that students felt that they "wanted to bolt from the class and rush to the railway station to get a ticket to China or Indonesia."

It went like this.

"If you see ten men trying to move a log," Gus would say, "and nine of the men are on one end and only one on the other, which side would you help? Obviously, it would be the one with the greater need. Apply this to missions. The United States, with seven percent of the world's population, has ninety percent of the world's preachers. Ninety-three percent of the world's population has only seven percent of the world's preachers and missionaries!"

Gus' students delighted in his instruction. Perhaps this can best be illustrated by the following tribute written to and presented to Gus at the close of one of his classes during the term of 1947-48:

> Seven individuals have spent seven happy weeks together in Classroom Four. We have been drawn together from several walks of life, from many points on the continent, for a variety of reasons, perhaps. Six of us entered the classroom timidly, inquiringly, openly to study a course in Missions. You, Mr. Woerner, have been not only our teacher but our leader and spiritual adviser. From the moment we entered the room and bowed in prayer till that bell sent us reluctantly away, you have led us into closer fellowship with Christ and inspired us with a desire to make His gospel known in the

dark and needy mission fields of the earth.

We just want you to know that you have made a tremendous impact on our lives in the interest of missions. You have supplied many, many answers to our questioning minds. Your personal experiences have made your theories live.

We do pray that the continued blessing of our Heavenly Father, the leadership and guidance of the Holy Spirit, and the presence and peace of our Lord Jesus Christ might continue with you always. Amen.

Yours in Christ's bonds,
Goldie Blakeney and the other five*

The TFC missions program was attracting many students. In fact, of the eighteen students who graduated from the high school in the spring of 1950, twelve came back to take the college courses. And of the 183 students in the college division, 85 were missions majors. That same year, nine graduates were commissioned to the four corners of the earth by various mission boards.

Meanwhile, the Woerners moved to a lovely cottage which was being renovated for use as a

* Goldie served as a missionary in Nigeria from 1948 to 1990. She now teaches conversational English to missionary candidates in South Korea. Most of the others also went overseas.

guest house. Built across the road from Gate Cottage, it was situated on the ash heap where Haddock Inn, the original campus building that burned in 1913, had once stood. Pauline became the hostess of the guest house.

One of the deepest desires of the Woerners was that at least one of their children would heed the call to the mission field. Can you imagine their pleasure when all three of them became missionaries?

"To have three children and all of them go to the mission field is nothing short of the grace of God and a miracle," wrote Gus. "We do not take any credit for it. True, their parents were missionaries. The children were dedicated as infants to the Lord and to missionary service, if that would be the Lord's will. They knew our wishes and prayers for them; therefore, we prayed that our lives, though weak and imperfect, might not be a hindrance to any of them in any way to thwart the will of God in their lives."

## Robert George Woerner

When Robert was about nine years old, he wrote from Hong Kong to his parents in Poseh that he had given his heart to Jesus. Then, when his parents were in Malaya and Robert in Elberta, he wrote (at age thirteen): "At a revival meeting, I dedicated my life to the Lord to be a missionary to China."

After the family moved to Toccoa Falls, Gus had the unique privilege of having Robert—and later Ruth and Raymond—in his doctrine and missions classes. In 1948, Robert graduated from TFI with a major in missions.

All along Robert felt led to return as a missionary to China where he had been born. Since the communists had overrun China and all foreign missionaries had been expelled, that door was closed. At first, he was very disappointed. Later, when the Alliance was looking for two single men to pioneer in New Guinea (now Irian Jaya) Robert volunteered. The candidates must be willing, the board said, to serve the Lord for five years before getting married. Robert consulted his fiancée; she agreed to wait. Thus, in 1952, armed with the prayers of his parents, friends and supporting churches, Robert left for New Guinea.

However, finding the work demanding and beyond his level of endurance, he suffered a nervous breakdown and had to return home for treatment at a Georgia state hospital.

Several times Gus and Pauline took him out of the hospital and cared for him at home. At one point they even decided to resign their positions at Toccoa and move to Elberta, hoping that a familiar environment might help him. However, he did not improve, and they found it necessary to return him to the hospital. Dr. Bandy was quick to invite the Woerners back to TFI. For most of the succeeding years, Robert lived in various homes for the disabled. Though his physical condition deteriorated, he maintained a good memory and witnessed for Christ—and often reminisced about his time in New Guinea.

In 1976, Robert moved to a nursing home near Elberton, about sixty-five miles from Toccoa. His sister, Ruth, and her husband, Charles, visited him faithfully about once a month. Just before Thanksgiving of 1996, Bob had a stroke after which he was confined to a wheelchair and had difficulty speaking. This was followed by bouts of pneumonia. On March 10, 1997, he went to be with the Lord.

## Ruth Woerner Good

On June 5, 1950, Ruth Woerner and Charles Good exchanged wedding vows in the college chapel on the evening after she graduated from TFI. Charles had graduated one year earlier. It was also her parents' silver wedding anniversary.

Ruth and Charles applied to The Christian and Missionary Alliance for service in Peru. They, along with Ruth's brother Ray and their families, left for the field on the same day in 1955. After studying Spanish in Costa Rica for a year, the Goods proceeded to Peru, and Ray and his wife Betty Jean went to Chile.

Ruth and Charles served the Lord as Alliance missionaries in Peru from 1955 to 1966. At first in Trujillo, then in other cities, they engaged in church planting. In one city, Charles superintended the construction of a new church building. He also had a thirty-minute radio program twice a week. Using a modern version of the New Testament, he taught English during the first fifteen minutes and preached in Spanish the rest of the half hour. In addition, both he and Ruth taught in the Bible school.

In 1966, as Ruth and Charles were preparing to leave on furlough, Ruth felt God was telling her that they would not return: "If thou wilt be perfect, go and sell that thou hast, and give to the poor, and thou shalt have treasure in heaven: and come and follow me" (Matthew 19:21).

The words "go and sell that thou hast, and give to the poor" came into her mind over and over as she was beginning to pack. Finally, she told Charles that she could have no peace until they followed God's instructions. At first, he did not understand, but they eventually sold everything, including their car, and gave the money to the Peruvian Church. They came home practically penniless.

The following year, near the end of their furlough, Dr. Bandy, then president of TFI, asked Charles to teach at the college.

"There are few missionaries with a master's degree and qualified to teach in a Bible college," noted Bandy. (Charles later earned his doctorate.) Ruth was asked to become the director of the school library. She and Charles have served

at Toccoa Falls in teaching and other capacities
including Director of Counseling, Testing and
Job Placement (Charles), and Head Librarian,
Director of Readers' Services and Head Archi-
vist until retirement in 1998 (Ruth).

## *Raymond Paul Woerner*

Ray and his wife Betty Jean were called to
Chile in 1955 as teachers in the Alliance Bible
School in Temuco. In 1974, they, with their four
children, returned to TFC on an extended furlough. Ray worked in the financial aid department. Betty Jean became secretary to TFC
president, Dr. Kenn Opperman.

When Gus heard that Ray and his family were
coming to the States, he and Pauline vacated
their home on the lower campus and moved to a
smaller place near the center of the upper campus in order to provide accommodations for Ray
and his family.

It was the first week of November 1977. It
had been raining for days and nights on end.
And still the rain fell. People were becoming un-
easy, especially those living in the low area below the main campus buildings—student
families in mobile homes and faculty and staff
members in brick homes along Toccoa Creek.

Betty Jean Woerner, Ray's wife, was nervous
too as she thought about Kelly Barnes Lake
above the 186-foot-high drop of Toccoa Falls.
The lake was contained by an earthen dam 500

feet long, 60 feet thick and 26 feet high. Betty knew that four mature students constantly monitored the dam. Surely there was no cause for alarm.

In the early hours of November 6, 1977, the water had risen to only one foot below the level of their home. Concerned about the family car, at 1:15 a.m. Betty Jean woke her son David and asked him to move it to higher ground.

At that moment there was a sound like thunder and all campus lights went out. The earthen dam on Kelly Barnes Lake had burst!

Denise, one of Ray and Betty Jean's daughters, grabbed her clothes and dressed, then began running past other trailers, thumping on them and calling out the news. Eventually she reached higher ground.

By now, the other four—Betty Jean, her daughter Deborah and her sons David and Daniel—were outside, trying to stay together by holding onto a floating car. But when a thirty-foot wall of water, traveling at approximately 120 miles per hour hit, the group was thrown apart. The boys swam and finally made their way through the debris-filled torrent to higher ground.

Ray was working in town that night. When he got off work at 3 a.m. and neared the campus, he was unable to cross the bridge over Toccoa Creek. There was water everywhere. Chillingly, in the murky darkness, he saw his own trunk float by, the one he'd had in Chile. By the time the boys found him, Debbie and Betty Jean were at a nearby hospital—in the morgue.

Several years went by before Ray could even think of going back to Chile where he and Betty Jean had worked together for twenty years. Instead, he began broadcasting with Frank Nagle, the "Night Watchman" at the campus radio station WRAF. Gradually, the possibilities and potential of Christian radio in Chile began to build in his soul. What a ministry it could be!

One night, at a banquet in Anderson, South Carolina, he voiced his desire to start such a station. The next day, a lady sent him a check for $1,000. From that moment on, a series of miracles—approval of the license, funds to buy equipment, nationals to build and run the station, duty-free importation of equipment and increased wattage—led to the inception of radio station HOPE (*Esperanza* in Spanish), the first and only Christian station in all of Chile.

Since 1985 there has been a miraculous expansion of the facilities. Now, Radio HOPE broadcasts over three stations daily. Although Ray retired officially in 1996, he is still active in radio work in Chile. Also, on March 8, 1997, he married a lovely Chilean woman, Estrellita Schulz, who helps him at the station and serves as a Spanish announcer.

Certainly, for the Woerners, missions was and is a family affair.

# 17

# *Blessings Accrue*

For several years, Gus and Pauline lived in the guest house on the lake and became its hosts. Pauline was particularly suited to such a ministry. Always adaptable and with a genuine love for people, she was described by some as a "classy, fancy china, polished silver" kind of person. When not occupied with guests, Pauline also helped in the alumni office, print shop and mailing department of TFI, spoke to women's groups and at times went on missionary convention tours. The Woerners' role of hospitality allowed them fellowship with many interested friends and alumni of the school as well as visiting faculty, special lecturers and others.

Gus too had ministry opportunities apart from the college, including twelve years teaching a class at the First Methodist Church in Toccoa and fourteen years at an evening Bible class in the Broad River Baptist Church near Baldwin, about twenty-two miles from the Institute.

When Dr. and Mrs. Bandy moved to Toccoa Falls and needed housing, the Woerners moved once more to allow the Bandys the only facility large enough to care for their family. Gus and Pauline took up residence in Earl Cottage, not far down the creek.

Later when the Woerners moved back to Toccoa Falls after their brief time in Elberta with Robert, the problem of housing faced them once again. No faculty homes were available.

Gus approached Dr. Bandy.

"If we can sell our place in Elberta, we will build a house on campus," he told him. The idea met with Dr. Bandy's approval.

In a surprisingly short time, Paul, one of their nephews, offered to buy the farm. The value of real estate had almost doubled since they had bought it in 1942. With the money, Gus was able to build a four-bedroom brick house on campus, complete with a reversion clause to Toccoa Falls College. It was that house that was occupied by Ray and his family when it was swept away in the flood of 1977.

While Gus was building the new home, he became concerned about facilities for other missionary families on furlough. He knew that many came home with no specific place to live. *Wouldn't it be wonderful*, he thought, *if Toccoa Falls had several missionary houses especially for*

*TFC graduates on furlough? Since the campus had more than 1,100 acres of land, mostly hills and valleys, there would surely be room for more residences—if funds and financing were available.* The faculty and staff thought it was a wonderful idea.

However, TFC, like most colleges, had always operated on a shoestring budget. Getting the necessary money could be a problem. Providentially, the TFC Alumni Association sponsored a special project each year. Hearing about Gus' vision, they decided to begin construction on a missionary house. The local lumber company agreed to build a three-bedroom house for a down payment of $2,000 and collect the rest as rent until the debt was paid in full. This became the first missionary residence, known as the Alumni Missionary House.

Meanwhile, Carolyn Woerner Eckman, Gus' niece (his brother Fred's youngest daughter), came home on furlough from Irian Jaya. With no place to stay, the family crowded into her husband David's parents' apartment. Gus decided he would try to raise $2,000 from Carolyn's brothers and sisters if permission could be obtained to build a second house on the same conditions as the first. The house became known as the Fred Woerner Missionary House.

Next, two homes were financed by Janie Carlisle (Hargrave), a longtime friend of the Forrests (Dr. Forrest was the founder of the Institute). The houses were named the Janie Carlisle House and the Janie Hargrave House.

About that time, Ray and his family were coming home from Chile. There was no place for them to live.

"If I raise $2,000 for a down payment," Gus asked Dr. Bandy, "will the school be willing to finance another missionary house?" Bandy agreed.

Gus and Pauline gave Dr. Bandy the first $500. With gifts from the Woerner family and other friends, over $5,000 came in. It became known as the Gus Woerner House.

Another house followed and the hill above the campus took on the name "Missionary Hill." Today a total of six homes for missionaries stand completely furnished and equipped, even to soap in the bathrooms and spices in the cupboard. The furloughing family has only to unpack their suitcases and they are "home."

A special blessing came to Gus in 1975. He often thought of his Indonesian students and wondered what had happened to them since he left the country. One of these was P.N. Potu, who had been a second-year student when the Woerners arrived in Makassar in 1936.

One day after class, Potu had come to Gus in his office.

"I thought I was a Christian," he said candidly, "but after your lecture today, I realize that I do not really know what it is to be saved. God spoke to me during the class and I am here to confess my ignorance and to repent of my sins. I want to accept Jesus Christ as my Savior and Lord."

Imagine Gus' surprise almost forty years later to read that P.N. Potu was the president of the entire Indonesian work of The Christian and Missionary Alliance.

In 1971, Pauline suffered a series of physical attacks: a case of shingles, an injury resulting from a car accident involving a high-speed impact from behind, a long siege of cystitis and finally a stroke followed by three more the following year. Her trials reminded Gus of James 1:2 which, translated into Chinese reads, "Count it all joy when ye fall into divers temptations." Her health continued to be unstable, her mind and hearing impaired.

When Dr. Bandy heard of the Woerners' plans to move to Florida, he approached Gus.

"You don't want to go to Florida. We want you to stay here. As long as you and your wife want to live at Toccoa Falls, you are welcome." Accordingly, they decided to remain and continue to do what they could to help the school.

On November 26, 1971, Gus celebrated his fiftieth year in the ministry. Among other tributes, the Gustave Woerner Missions Lecture Series Fund was established in his honor. Its purpose would be the advancing and perpetuating of foreign missions on the campus. This fund continues to enable the college to have an annual series of missionary lectures.

A plaque was also presented to the Woerners during the 1971 Homecoming. The standing ovation left them speechless. Then, in 1975 Gus officially retired. At the commencement exercises on May 9, the retiral of "Mr. Missionary" was announced. He responded with the words: "May 'God's Bible School,' as my mother called it, continue to flourish and bear much fruit for the glory of God, with emphasis on foreign missions, until Jesus comes, is my prayer."

Less than a month later, on June 5, 1975, Gus and Pauline celebrated their golden wedding anniversary. She was seventy-seven; he, seventy-nine. One of Gus' favorite words from the Bible was Ebenezer, which means "Hitherto hath the LORD helped us" (1 Samuel 7:12). In almost every prayer Gus prayed he used the word, and he often sang the hymn, "Come, Thou Fount of Every Blessing":

> Here I raise my Ebenezer,
> Hither by Thy help I'm come;
> And I hope, by Thy good pleasure,
> Safely to arrive at home.

# 18

# *Promoted to Glory*

I t was the evening of Wednesday, May 3, 1978. Uncle Gus was excited. Dr. Alvin Moser, academic dean of the college had asked him to pray the dedicatory prayer for twenty-one TFC students about to disburse to every corner of the globe as summer missionaries.

Gus was thrilled to be asked. During his tenure as missions instructor, he had seen more than 100 of his students accept God's call and go to the corners of the earth.

With the young people lined up across the front of the auditorium, Gus poured out his heart to God, praying earnestly and tenderly for these precious students. He had taught them and encouraged them in his classes, and his heart swelled with joy as they pledged themselves to reach others for Christ. By the time the Amen was breathed, a holy hush had fallen on the entire group. It was as if they had all been lifted into the heavenlies.

But Gus was not finished.

"Dr. David J. Fant has just completed a biography of our lives," he announced. "It will be off the press in two days. I'll be in Fant Hall between 2:30 and 4 on Sunday afternoon and will hand out free autographed copies to all students who come for them." The students, hardly noticing that their Uncle Gus looked very pale, gave him a rousing ovation.

The benediction was pronounced and most of the students left. Gus stepped down from the platform and together with Dr. Moser walked toward the back of the building. As they arrived at the last row of seats, Gus reached for a chair and slumped to the floor. Two staff nurses rushed to his side, but there was no pulse. The Rev. Gustave Woerner had gone into the presence of his Lord. What a beautiful conclusion to a consecrated life!

God gave him his wish to die with "his boots on" and "in the harness." Instead of an autograph session, family and friends gathered for his funeral service on Sunday afternoon at 2 p.m. Hundreds came to honor the man they called Uncle Gus, the one who had ministered to them in so many ways.

Dr. L.L. King, then president of The Christian and Missionary Alliance, related that a missionary once told him that Dr. Jaffray could never have done the work he did had it not been for Gustave Woerner. In his book on the life of Jaffray, Dr. A.W. Tozer wrote: "Jaffray . . . [had] one loyal disciple who would have followed him over a cliff if he commanded it. This was Gustave Woerner."

No one can measure on this side of eternity the impetus to missionary work and service contributed by this man, both on the mission field and as Professor of Missions at Toccoa Falls Institute. His influence has been worldwide.

While he was a student at Nyack, he wrote the following class song. He not only wrote it—he lived it.

### "Not I, But Christ"

Not I, but Christ, shall be exalted,
Not I, but Christ, be lifted up;
Not I, but Christ, shall have the glory,
'Twas He who drank the bitter cup.

*Chorus:*
Not I, but Christ; Not I, but Christ;
My constant prayer shall be.
Oh, crucify each vain desire,
And live Thy life in me.

Not I, but Christ, has wrought salvation,
Not I, but Christ, shall have the praise;
Not I, but Christ, can save the sinner,
And fill his soul with joyful lays.

Not I, but Christ, shall rule my being,
Not I, but Christ, direct my way:
Not I, but Christ, the new life living,
Of constant victory day by day.

Not I, but Christ, our glorious motto,
Not I, but Christ, our only theme;
Not I, but Christ, till ev'ry creature,
Shall own Him Lord and King supreme.

Pauline joined her husband in glory on November 8, 1978, just six months after Gus' homegoing. Together again.

They will never be forgotten. In 1996, the million-dollar Woerner School of World Missions Center was dedicated on the Toccoa Falls College campus. The center was partially funded by Edward J. Woerner and Sons in honor of the Woerner family, a number of whom have been or are now missionaries—one of the first having been Gustave Woerner.

David Woerner, Fred's oldest grandson, now a Methodist minister, spoke at the dedication.

"We have gathered to remember our roots and especially to honor our grandfather Fred and his brother, our Uncle Gus Woerner. I remember both men as being great men of prayer. I know of no other men who gave so much time to intercessory prayer. The success of the Woerner family is the result of their prayers.

"We need to stop for a moment and recall that there were two great women behind these two men—Grandma Emma and Aunt Pauline, daughters of God who loved Him very much. Both were prayer warriors throughout their lives."

> *Blessed are the dead which die in the Lord from henceforth: Yea, saith the Spirit, that they may rest from their labours; and their works do follow them. (Revelation 14:13)*

# Addenda

A. "Not I, But Christ"—written by Gustave Woerner.

B. "New Tribes Mission Takes over Ringlet from the Alliance."

C. Graph—Missions Graduates at Toccoa Falls College Since 1950.

## "Not I, but Christ"

Galatians 2:20

Class Song, 1923 Nyack Missionary Training Institute

Gustave Woerner

Robert Gilly

### New Tribes Mission Takes
### over Ringlet from the Alliance

The Cameron Highlands Bible School, under the direction of the Woerners, had gotten off to an auspicious start. Then Japan entered World War II. Japanese troops swept down the Malay Peninsula, forcing all missionaries to leave. Those who did not leave were interned in prison camps. Dr. Jaffray died there.

After the war ended, there were two Mission organizations which wanted to renew activities in Malaysia, The Christian and Missionary Alliance and the New Tribes Mission. Since it would be most satisfactory to have only one group in the area, in May 1948, the Alliance contacted the New Tribes Mission, notifying them that they approved their taking over the property at Ringlet. At that time, however, a division of the British government was using the property. Therefore, the New Tribes Mission could not occupy it.

In October 1949, New Tribes missionary Paul Linn visited Ringlet. He found many believers, some of whom he had baptized two years earlier. Only a caretaker lived on the school property.

Early in 1952 he made another trip. Since Paul Linn was Chinese, he was able to get through the communists who were still in control of the area.

As of 1997, the New Tribes Mission has a headquarters in Singapore and a representative in Penang, Malaysia.

(Information provided by the New Tribes Mission historian, Terence Sherwood.)

## Missions Graduates at
## Toccoa Falls College Since 1950*

| Year | Total Graduates | Missions Graduates | % Missions Graduates |
|------|-----------------|--------------------|----------------------|
| 50 | 54 | 0 | 0.0 |
| 51 | 36 | 1 | 2.8 |
| 52 | 41 | 1 | 2.4 |
| 53 | 23 | 0 | 0.0 |
| 54 | 42 | 0 | 0.0 |
| 55 | 44 | 0 | 0.0 |
| 56 | 41 | 0 | 0.0 |
| 57 | 28 | 0 | 0.0 |
| 58 | 43 | 14 | 32.6 |
| 59 | 36 | 0 | 0.0 |
| 60 | 27 | 7 | 25.0 |
| 61 | 31 | 15 | 48.4 |
| 62 | 27 | 11 | 40.7 |
| 63 | 33 | 10 | 30.3 |
| 64 | 23 | 12 | 52.2 |
| 65 | 23 | 11 | 47.8 |
| 66 | 21 | 13 | 61.9 |
| 67 | 22 | 2 | 9.1 |
| 68 | 42 | 20 | 47.6 |
| 69 | 38 | 12 | 31.6 |
| 70 | 54 | 20 | 37.0 |
| 71 | 37 | 9 | 24.3 |
| 72 | 39 | 13 | 33.3 |
| 73 | 30 | 10 | 33.3 |
| 74 | 39 | 8 | 20.5 |
| 75 | 45 | 10 | 22.2 |
| 76 | 56 | 13 | 23.2 |

| Year | Total Graduates | Missions Graduates | % Missions Graduates |
|------|-----------------|--------------------|----------------------|
| 77 | 62 | 12 | 19.4 |
| 78 | 46 | 12 | 26.1 |
| 79 | 67 | 12 | 17.9 |
| 80 | 79 | 21 | 26.6 |
| 81 | 92 | 18 | 19.6 |
| 82 | 72 | 18 | 25.0 |
| 83 | 96 | 18 | 18.8 |
| 84 | 106 | 16 | 15.1 |
| ' 85 | 116 | 18 | 15.5 |
| 86 | 112 | 19 | 17.0 |
| 87 | 91 | 12 | 13.2 |
| 88 | 95 | 10 | 10.5 |
| 89 | 98 | 13 | 13.3 |
| 90 | 127 | 18 | 14.2 |
| 91 | 134 | 18 | 13.4 |
| 92 | 162 | 23 | 14.2 |
| 93 | 168 | 18 | 10.7 |
| 94 | 161 | 11 | 6.8 |
| 95 | 175 | 17 | 9.1 |
| 96 | 168 | 16 | 9.5 |
| ** Total since 1950: | | | |
| | 3,203 | 531 | 16.6 |

* Gus Woerner began teaching Missions full-time at Toccoa Falls College in 1949. He retired officially in 1975.
** Information supplied by the Office of Institutional Research, Toccoa Falls College. Used by permission.